GAME CHANGER

THE CRUISE THAT CHANGED EVERYTHING

Philippians 3:13-14

Tommy Ferrell, Ph.D.

ISBN 978-0-578-62062-6

Published by Game Changer Books
Atlanta, Georgia

Printed in the United States of America

DEDICATION

Dedicated first to God who changed my game…second to Nancy Ferrell, a mother who prayed and sent care packages, and finally… to Elyse, Garrison, Joseph, and Bailey, whom I love.

CONTENTS

FOREWORD

It is a privilege and distinct honor to write this foreword for Doctor Tommy Ferrell, PhD, a missionary in God's Army for the past 33 years and currently the Lead Pastor of Briarlake Baptist Church in Decatur, Georgia. In 1985, as an 18-year-old sailor, Tommy served in the crew of my US Navy aircraft carrier, the USS *Saratoga*, (CV-60). There, the author experienced the rigors of daily life at sea on a supercarrier. Each day brings a new experience as Navy battle groups are always forward, on call for immediate response, near problem nations, and alert to rogue forces. This deployment was no exception and the author's life experiences became unique in many ways.

As I look back on my 37-year Navy career, I too experienced dramatic events in each segment of my Navy life. First, as a sailor fresh from high school, then as a carrier-based fighter pilot with multiple deployments to Vietnam, a fighter squadron commander, TOP GUN Training Squadron command, aircraft carrier command, and finally, battlegroup and fleet command. The most demanding, yet satisfying, of these opportunities was as Tommy's Commanding Officer on the USS *Saratoga*. It is in the job description of an aircraft carrier to carry out nationally directed emerging tasks in support of America's security, to conduct air and sea intercepts of hostile forces, to maintain freedom of the seas, and to defend the United States and her allies.

At times, as directed by our National Command Authority, hostile forces are engaged, and our highly trained warriors accomplish their missions under very specific rules of engagement. Such was the case on the USS *Saratoga* in 1985-86. Within the crew of the *Saratoga*, there was a small number of highly trained sailors, selected for their special abilities and qualities, known as Operations Specialists. Such was Tommy Ferrell's assignment - on the bridge, on lookout observation stations, and in the Combat Information Center, which is the nerve center of the ship for all tactical operations - his front row seat!

This was the basis for Tommy's life changing experiences as a young sailor on a supercarrier. I can personally relate to his scenario. I too joined the Naval Reserve at age 17 before shipping out at age 18. After my initial training and just into my first assignment, a 3-star Admiral sent me to Flight School and allowed me to bypass the college requirement. I never forgot my beginnings as a sailor in the crackerjack uniform. Conventional wisdom says: "Don't be friends with your sailors as the Captain." Wrong! It was always my experience that trust and camaraderie make a winning team!

This book, GAME CHANGER, records through the author's eyes the deployed operations on an aircraft carrier. He focuses primarily on operations against Libya in the Gulf of Sidra, commonly known as crossing "The Line of Death," as well as the capture of the *Achille Lauro* cruise ship by terrorists. In addition to these well publicized events, there were a number of other situations to which we responded. These included: the German night club bombing which killed two US servicemen and the hijacking of the TWA airliner where a Navy Seabee Diver, Robert Stethem, was shot, killed, and then dumped on the tarmac in Beirut, Lebanon. Petty Officer Stethem had two brothers in the Navy at that time, one of whom served with us on the *Saratoga*!

In addition, the *Saratoga* conducted the first ever nighttime transit of the Suez Canal, as we passed from the Mediterranean into the Indian Ocean! Once there, we were directed to attempt the first-ever tie-up of a carrier to the pier at the remote military base Diego Garcia in the Indian Ocean. Though we accomplished this feat successfully, it will not likely be repeated due to the keel depth of a carrier and the relatively shallow water in the harbor at Diego Garcia.

The author has captured the spirit of the "Mighty Fine" sailors onboard the *Saratoga*. This was a spirit fostered first by President, Ronald Reagan. The President was fully aware of the military actions of the USS *Saratoga* during our deployment and, at times, involved closely through his National Security Advisor, former Marine Bud McFarland. At times, we were in direct contact with the Situation Room at the White House, as President Reagan was closely monitoring the successes of the *Saratoga*. Yes, it was an eventful deployment for all of us!

Vice Admiral Jerry Unruh, USN (ret)

ACKNOWLEDGEMENTS

What began as a week of post-international travel-related stomach-illness, turned into an unexpected opportunity to write the book, GAME CHANGER: *The Cruise that Changed Everything*. In short, I had some time on my hands over the 4th of July holiday as I could not venture far from the facilities for about a week and that condition resulted in the beginning of this book. They say God works in mysterious ways, and this book is certainly a testament to that cliché.

Over the years, I have often reflected upon, and spoken of, my experience on the *Saratoga* as it relates specifically to my "call to the ministry." For a pastor, one's call to the ministry is a defining experience and mine occurred initially on board the USS *Saratoga* during its 1985-86 Med/IO deployment. I had not reflected upon, nor said much about, the larger context of what I experienced and what the crew collectively accomplished during that deployment. For whatever reason, during the past year the events of that deployment, their significance in my life, and well as the larger role this cruise played in the life of our nation, has increasingly occupied my thoughts.

Having two nineteen-year old sons in college and observing the differences between their lives and mine, when I was nineteen years old on the *Saratoga*, brought forth a range of emotions. I realized that the experience of young college students and that of young enlistees in the armed services could not be more different. In addition, my awareness has grown of the visible, and invisible, wounds our veterans return with from what began as The War on Terror after September 11, 2001. This past Memorial Day, for whatever reason, I was particularly sensitive to those who have sacrificed so much for our freedoms. My heart particularly goes out to those who enlist at a young age and are so soon deployed to areas of conflict and combat responsibilities. Since the earliest days of our nation, young men, and more recently young women as well, have stepped up to defend our nation in the early-blossoming prime of their lives.

Given all of these factors, it seemed the right thing to do to tell what it was like for me, and for so many others who served. Other young men on the USS *Saratoga* with whom I served would likely agree that our military service was, to quote Charles Dickens, "the best of times and the worst of times." I am grateful for these men and have managed to keep contact with a few such as Larry Thompson, Lee Shonfelt, Alfonso Conti, Timothy Wallace and Joseph Blake, all of whom served with me in OI Division on the USS *Saratoga*. These are just a few of the many who gave their younger years to their country. Like them, I received much in return; even perhaps more than I realize.

To those who have helped me bring this book to fruition through suggestions, proofreading, and encouragement; I am grateful. My wife, Elyse Sanderlin Ferrell, tops the list. My administrative assistant Shirley Poulton and other Briarlake Church members have been helpful including Sylvia Daughtry, David & Tricia Roberts, Charlie Crook, Marlene Green, and the list could go on. Jess Rainer, of Craft Book Publishing, has been helpful with encouragement and advice. Andrew Snowden, of Timeless Tattoo in Atlanta, gave valued assistance to the book jacket design.

One of the high pleasures of my life has been the recent opportunity to reconnect and spend meaningful time in conversation with Vice-Admiral Jerry Unruh, my former commanding officer on the USS *Saratoga*. His life as a naval officer, with such a significant and successful command resume, should be studied by those who aspire to military leadership. After the passing of thirty-two years, it has been a great privilege to reacquaint myself with this man, our commander, whom I admired so much as one young sailor among 5,000 on the USS *Saratoga*. To all those throughout the ranks of our military who lead well, like Admiral Unruh, and to those who follow – we owe a debt of gratitude.

INTRODUCTION

As newly minted sailors fresh from boot camp in the late summer of 1984, we were stepping onto the streets of a nation with mixed feelings about the military, to put it mildly. Post-Vietnam anti-military sentiment lingered, and the U.S. had been on a long losing streak since achieving an unprecedented victory of global scope in 1945, with the conclusion of World War II. During the eight months of the 1985-86 Mediterranean/Indian Ocean deployment (Med/IO) of the aircraft carrier USS *Saratoga*, however, the nation seemed to experience a change in its morale. As the widely publicized events of the *Saratoga's* Med/IO Cruise unfolded, for the first time in a long time, America was standing firmly behind her armed forces. That the country has largely supported its military in the passing years since the time of the Saratoga's deployment, a closer look at this transitional era is all the more interesting.

The *Saratoga* led in two major military and geopolitical incidents that together, contributed to a game changing climate in American culture, particularly in terms of its morale and patriotism. In October of 1985, an armed terrorist cell of the Palestinian Liberation Front (PLF) highjacked the Italian cruise ship *Achille Lauro*. Frustrated that their demands for Israel to release Palestinian prisoners were not being met, the hijackers shot and killed an elderly Jewish-American passenger named Leon Klinghoffer who was confined to a wheelchair. After his slaying, Mr. Klinghoffer's body was dumped overboard into the Mediterranean Sea as his grieving wife and frightened co-passengers watched in horror. This brazen act of terror made the unfolding hostage crisis all the more alarming. After negotiating safe passage on an Egyptian commercial jetliner, the terrorists were intent upon making their escape by air to Tunisia.

However, a Tunisian landing for the PLF terrorists was not in the cards. Instead, F-14 fighter jets from the USS *Saratoga* intercepted the commercial jetliner which had been commandeered by the terrorists, and forced it to land on a North Atlantic Treaty Organization (NATO) airbase in Sicily. That Seal Team Six was on station awaiting the terrorists, only added gravitas to the situation. Ultimately, the terrorists were quickly apprehended. after the forced landing, without shots being fired. On behalf of a grateful nation, President Ronald Reagan publicly congratulated the officers and men of the *Saratoga* as major media outlets from coast to coast reported the happenings of the *Achille Lauro* incident.

The second significant event for the officers and crew of the *Saratoga* occurred toward the end of the deployment in April 1986. By that time, the *Saratoga* had been designated as the flag ship of a three-carrier battle group consisting of approximately 75 U.S. Navy war ships and 210 Navy aircraft. This massive armada of naval vessels, aircraft, and armament would be tested in the largest sea battle since World War II. The *Saratoga* battle group would engage the Libyan Navy after Libyan provocations, including threats against the United States and live fire against naval assets that were protected by maritime law in international waters.

But beyond Libya, the greater existential threat at the time was the Soviet Union. The so-called "Cold War" between the post-World War II superpowers had quickly evolved into a series of proxy shooting wars between nations subordinate to the Soviet Union and, thus, turned against the United States. From Korea, to Vietnam, to Lebanon, and Libya, the Soviets equipped and armed proxy states in their attempt to spread an atheistic totalitarian one party system, specifically Communism, around the globe. In 1986, the *Saratoga* battle group would disable and destroy three Soviet made Libyan flagged naval warships of the "Nanuchka" class, as well as several shore-based early warning radar sites operated by the Libyan Military on Libyan soil.

The fact that Soviet warships were operating in this particular area, the Gulf of Sidra, at the time of the Libyan Conflict, made the possibility of an armed escalation between the two superpowers very real. When warplanes of the *Saratoga* battle group crossed Qaddafi's Line of Death along the 32' 30' parallel, some two hundred miles from Libya's coastline, on April 15, 1986, the possibility of a nuclear war with the Soviet Union was at high tide. That the Soviet Union did not come to the aid of their proxy force, the Libyan Navy, when they were successfully counterattacked by the U.S. Navy, was a major win for the United States of America. In fact, historians mark the second half of the 1980s as the beginning of the dissolution of the Soviet Union. The rise of militant Islam would also characterize and follow this era of the_*Saratoga*'s storied cruise and the collapse of the Soviet Union. It is indisputable that the 1985-86 deployment of the *Saratoga* was, among other factors, a gamechanger in the larger scheme of significant things that were unfolding in the world at that time.

This book is an attempt to put these occurrences of the *Sarato-*

ga's 1985-86 Med/IO deployment in their larger historical context so as to better evaluate their significance. As a nineteen-year old Operations Specialist working in the Combat Information Center during her 1985-86 deployment, I was both a bystander and an active participant in the things that took place. Indeed, the entire crew was essential to the success of the *Saratoga*. Every sailor and marine in the entire *Saratoga* battle group was vital to her success. But from the nerve center of the ship, known as the Combat Information Center, or CIC, operations specialists were involved in a wide range of activities from the routine navigation of the ship to providing combat related information to the Tactical Action Officer, as well as feeding vital information to the ship's captain himself. Looking back on this particular deployment, and all things considered, it is not an overstatement to assert that the *Saratoga*'s 1985-86 deployment was indeed the cruise that changed everything. For doubters, perhaps the following pages of the book will prove to be persuasive.

Yet my greater purpose in relaying the facts and observations of this significant time period is to tell the story of a spiritual awakening that occurred, specifically, upon the *Saratoga* during this eight-month cruise. The baptism of over one hundred of *Saratoga*'s crew in the Jordan River on 09 November 1985, during a port visit to Haifa, Israel early in the cruise, is a measurable indication of the spiritual currents that were bearing upon this body of sailors. This spiritual awakening would markedly affect to some degree, directly or indirectly, the entire 5,000-man crew and airwing.

It seemed that no squadron, division, or compartment of the ship was without some evidence and indication that a spiritual awakening was widespread among the crew as a whole. It was common to see sailors with *Our Daily Bread* devotional booklets in their dungaree shirt pockets and Gideon pocket New Testaments, including

Psalms and Proverbs, in the back pockets of their duty uniforms. Spiritual conversations were common on the mess decks. Racial relations among whites, blacks, Asians, and Hispanics were very positive and we all got along like a big family. This is not to say there weren't family squabbles, but conflict always gave way to the overarching climate of positive regard and adherence to the mission that was so essential to living in close quarters on a sea-going warship.

My recollection is that interpersonal relations, in general, were positive on the *Saratoga*. Like almost all large organizations, including the United States Navy, a positive *esprit de corps* is not to be taken for granted. When such a positive demeanor is evident, you can usually draw a direct correlation to the primary leader of the organization. Much of the credit, humanly speaking, for the positive climate onboard *Saratoga* undoubtedly goes to the ship's commanding officer, Captain Jerry L. Unruh.

By the time that Captain Unruh assumed command in April 1985, he had already served his country as a fighter pilot in the Vietnam War, commanded a fighter squadron, served as Commanding Officer of the Navy's Top Gun School in Miramar, California, and he had commanded a deep draft vessel, which is a prerequisite to assuming the command of an aircraft carrier. Of all of his innate strengths, in addition to his extraordinary resume of life experiences, it is my recollection that his positive demeanor and high regard for his country and crew were among the most evident characteristics that marked his leadership style while in command of the *Saratoga* from 1985-87.

It is with great appreciation that I recently reconnected with Vice Admiral Jerry Unruh (Ret.) thirty-three years after our 1985-86 deployment. He is nearly eighty years old, still married to Dee, and is actively involved with his family and community. He even pilots a seagoing vessel christened the *Mighty Fine*, which was his trademark expression to the crew over the 1 MC announcing system when things were going well, and they usually were. Since I was only eighteen years old when I received orders to join the crew of the *Saratoga*, all that I experienced on the ship in those days contributed significantly to the man I am today. The things I experienced on the *Saratoga* left a distinct mark upon me personally. In a book about his military experience, one of the founding members of the U.S. Army's Delta Force wrote: "The military is a profession that brands itself on the soul and causes you forever after to view the world through a unique set of mental filters. The more profound and intense the experience, the hotter the brand, and the deeper it is plunged into you."[1]

Undoubtedly, the things experienced by the officers and crew of the *Saratoga* were significant to each one of us in different ways. Collectively, however, few, if any, would deny that we were part of something bigger than ourselves. After much thoughtful consideration and historical research, I am convinced that this deployment was a game changer for our nation. Support for members of the military improved markedly. Our collective national morale improved. The country seemed to be lifted up and above its differences. The uniqueness of my experience, which led to a very personal and enduring sense of call to the gospel ministry in my life, is interwoven into the larger story of my time on the *Saratoga*.

Since separating from the *Saratoga* on 10 May 87, I continued the pursuit of my call to the ministry by furthering my education and serving in various church and denominational positions along the way. I have served my present church, Briarlake Baptist Church in Decatur, Georgia, as Senior Pastor since 2004. It is clear to me that my thirty-three years in the gospel ministry had its origin in the spiritual awakening that occurred on the *Saratoga* in 1985-86.

This revival movement had a significant impact upon me and many others. In a recent phone conversation with *Saratoga's* Command Chaplain, Hugo Hammond, during our 1985-86 deployment, he recalled fondly: "We definitely had revival on the *Saratoga*.[2] Many people would agree that we, as a nation, could use an uplifting spiritual awakening in our day. It is my hope that we can go beyond the divisiveness that has increasingly characterized our country at least as far back as the early 21st century. With over three decades spent in ministry since leaving the Navy, I can say with certainty that my time on the *Saratoga* was a real game changer in my life. For me, this was the cruise that changed everything. Here is my story.

CHAPTER 1

WATER, WATER, EVERYWHERE!

Coming up from the chilly water in the Jordan River on 09 November 1985 was an experience that I will never forget. I had just been immersed by a US Navy chaplain in the name of the Father, the Son, and the Holy Spirit. Just a few days before, I had been standing watch on the upper observation deck looking through the big eyes, which magnified the coastline of Beirut, Lebanon. As an operations specialist (OS) on the aircraft carrier USS *Saratoga*, my duties usually kept me in the ship's combat information center (CIC) where data on the various ships and aircraft in our operating area was observed by surface warfare officers and enlisted OSs of various rank.

When the ship was at sea, the constant surveillance of the surface, air, and subsurface picture was our responsibility to ensure the safe navigation of the ship and to provide timely and relevant information for tactical decision-making required of the TAO (tactical action officer) in the face of threats and hostilities. Ultimately, we provided information that assisted in the decision making of the ship's captain himself. As enlisted OSs, our responsibilities included the tracking of all contacts; whether friendly, hostile, or unknown. After nine-weeks of boot camp, including an initial orientation week, those who were designated to the job specification known as "operations specialists," moved on to a demanding seventeen-week school called OS "A" school, which was based at Dam Neck Fleet Combat Training Center Atlantic (FCTCLANT). Dam Neck was an out of the way place on the Atlantic Ocean in close proximity to Virginia Beach, Virginia. It has since received quiet acclaim as the home base of the Navy's Special Development Group (or DEVGRU); better known as SEAL TEAM 6.

Graduation day for OS "A" school was, for the most part, a rather subdued internal affair. There was no great pomp and circumstance as it was really just another steppingstone in our journey to the fleet. The highlight of graduation, as I recall, was that we were given our orders to our eventual duty station. Each of us was a bundle of nerves as this was seen as an epic moment of fate. As I recall, our class rank was the primary determining factor in our range of choices; first in class got first choice on the open billets and second in rank had the second grab. In most cases, graduating students in my class chose duty stations in proximity to their hometowns as, by this time, everyone seemed to be pretty homesick. Out of maybe twenty students, I was somewhere around the middle of the class as I recall. Choosing the USS *Saratoga*, an aircraft carrier out of Mayport, Florida looked pretty good to me. I was warned that carriers definitely go to sea, and that an aircraft carrier would be the first target of choice for the Soviets in any armed conflict. But, at eighteen years old that didn't give me any pause. At least I got to go to Florida and, at that time, the incentives outweighed the risks.

With our choices weighed in for consideration, the instructors made the final confirmation in the breath-holding ceremony that we had anticipated for at least 17 weeks. Of course, the instructors added their commentary and vast seagoing insight to this epic moment. This revelation of our next duty station took place in the manner of the unveiling of some great work of art. It was rather like the game show where the announcer calls another lucky contestant to "come on down...you are the next contestant on The Price is Right!" As I recall, it went something like this: "A round of applause everybody! Seaman Smith will be joining the smelly crew of a rusty Gator-Freighter out of Timbuktu!" A "Gator Freighter" is Navy and Marine Corp slang for an Amphibious Landing Ship. "Petty Officer Hernandez will be sunning his buns on shore duty in Key West, Florida." "Jones, you are going to have a do-over on OS "A" School for excessive stupidity. Just kidding...you have been selected to operate radar on an ice breaker in the Arctic Circle! Ha-Ha-Ha!"

Then my turn: "Ferrell, you are going to Mayport, Florida – there are a lot of shark attacks down there – and you are joining the USS *Saratoga*, a floating bullseye...good luck!" I can't recall exactly; but it went something along those lines. You can see why the day seemed so weighty to young men barely two decades old who were learning their fate for the next two-to-four years of their lives. I had no sense, whatsoever, of the adventures and, more importantly, the spiritual discoveries that awaited me.

For many of us, graduation from OS "A" school simply meant that we had to jump through one more hoop. In other words, we had one rung of the training ladder yet to climb. I was assigned to attend CV (Carrier Vessel) Data Input School, also at Dam Neck, since I was given orders to join with the OI (Operations Intelligence) Division of the aircraft carrier USS Saratoga, with homeport in Mayport, Florida. While things certainly could have been worse, I remember being jealous of two of my classmates in particular. One had orders to BUD/S (Basic Underwater Demolition/Seal) training at the Naval Amphibious Base at Coronado, California. The other had orders to OI Division on a Navy Cruiser out of Pearl Harbor, Hawaii. In retrospect, given all that I was soon to experience on the *Saratoga*, I do not think I would change places with either one of them. Looking back upon it all, it is now clear to me that God was directing my steps even though I was unaware at the time.

At sea, operations specialists worked eight hours on followed by eight hours off. And that cycle was repeated, ad nauseum; unless of course we were called to General Quarters Battle Stations either as a drill or in a real-time situation such as we would experience in the Gulf of Sidra more than two hundred miles off of the coast of Libya. In such cases; your duty would be extended as needed. During the eight hours off, you might be assigned other duties like cleaning, and of course "swabbing the decks" of your berthing compartment as well as the surrounding passageways that made a seagoing navy ship feel somewhat like a corn maze at Halloween. Due to this obsessive-compulsive propensity to keep the decks clean comes the light-hearted, but derogatory, navy-nickname "Swabbies." Sailors are often referred to as "swabbies" by members of the other military branches. When you are at sea on a Navy ship, however, neglect of the smallest details can result in disaster. Therefore, from stem to stern, Navy ships are purposefully kept in the best of order and preparedness.

In the eight consecutive hours OS's had off duty at sea, we had to eat, sleep, take care of individual concerns like laundry, personal hygiene, exercise, and any hobbies or activities that helped to maintain sanity. The *Saratoga*, as a large aircraft carrier with an accompaniment of 5,000 men, had a library, chapel, basketball courts in the hangar bay which were available when aircraft were not being moved about, two small gyms for weightlifting, and a flight deck that was over three hundred yards long. If the flight deck was not in use for flight ops, it was a great place to unwind and get some fresh air and needed exposure to the sun. I ran many a mile on that flight deck and there is no more beautiful background anywhere than the open sea or the mysterious coastline of some foreign nation as viewed from the flight deck of an aircraft carrier underway.

As a young OS just coming up through the ranks, I was regularly assigned a two-hour rotation to the Ship's Bridge during my eight hours on watch. The OSs responsibility on the Bridge was to maintain a surface contact plot-board for the ship's captain and the officer of the deck (OOD). Another entry level watch station for a 19-year old OS like me was the two-hour duty assignment as a look out on an observation deck above the bridge. Unless it was foul weather, one of my favorite reprieves from long hours in CIC was standing look out on the observation deck where we were to relay surface, sub-surface, or air-contact observations to CIC. You never knew when the periscope of a Soviet submarine that had gone undetected might peek above the surface. Even surfaced subs were inherently difficult to locate, due to their low-lying profile and virtual invisibility to radar. Under water, they were even more elusive.

Whether on watch in CIC, on the bridge, or as lookout on the upper exposed observation deck, the Operations Specialist was always connected to a larger communication network onboard ship through the medium of sound-powered phones. Bearings and ranges to surface contacts were called out from the OS who was watching the surface radar scope; while surface board plotters in CIC and on the bridge plotted the surface contacts relative to *Saratoga's* position. Lookouts increased the level of vigilance by maintaining visual surveillance of the surrounding surface and air theater so as to note and relay anything out of the ordinary. The intensity of the cold war conflict with the Soviet Union and the possibility of contact with their fleet and aircraft always kept us on our toes, especially when deployed with the Sixth Fleet in the Mediterranean Sea.

All of this data was gathered and evaluated to equip the captain, as well as the officer-of-the-deck, for the safe navigation of the ship. In addition, the same information that was routed to the Bridge was displayed in CIC for the benefit of the OSs, Ops Officers, and the TAO who worked in CIC, which was the nerve center of the ship. All the while, one half of the CIC crew was focused on the surface picture; the other half, especially on an aircraft carrier, was focused on the air picture. Operations Specialists, and the operations officers with whom they worked, were tasked with vectoring combat aircraft to areas of concern for surveillance and/or engagement of threats. It was the task of those of us in CIC to determine the identification of surface and air contacts as either friend or foe (IFF). The ultimate purpose was to enable the command structure to direct our air assets in the tactical engagement of hostile air or surface contacts as needed. Throw in sonar operations for submarine detection and tracking along with the fire control elements that are in place to deploy our ship's munitions and you have Combat Information Center in a nutshell. OSs were one of several different ratings within the Operations Department that made all of this work like clockwork on a super carrier.

As a young OS, all of this was interesting, but I always loved being outdoors. Consequently, the hours I spent on the observation deck as a lookout were some of my favorite times of duty. There was something very powerful and inspiring about being perched upon such a lofty position as the observation deck above the bridge overlooking the entire flight deck and air wing operation. With the help of the so-called "Big Eyes" binoculars, it was possible to see fifty miles to the horizon on a clear day.

As we steamed off the coast of Lebanon, however, no one needed the "Big Eyes" to see that Beirut was a mess. Beyond the crystalline blue waters of the eastern Mediterranean, you could see smoke plumes of various colors. Some smoke was dark black from the burning of tires, while other incendiaries emitted gray smoke, and then there were occasional flares of luminescent color. The staccato sound of automatic weapons firing never stopped for very long. Dat-Dat-Dat-Dat-Dat...over and over again. The buildings of this once beautifully developed city, formerly known as the French Riviera of the Middle East, had become pockmarked with bullet holes. Some of the structures were missing segments, with entire levels reduced to rubble. In those days, Beirut, Lebanon was a hot mess.

Lebanon, itself, is bordered to the south by Israel. Both countries have a strategic value disproportionate to their small geographic footprint due to their location along the eastern shore of the Mediterranean Sea and their proximity to the Arab World and all of its oil. In addition to its southern neighbor, Israel, Lebanon was completely enveloped on all points west and north by its ever-encroaching neighbor Syria. By the time that *Saratoga* was steaming off the coast of Lebanon in 1985, the vicious civil war there had been underway for ten long years since 1975, and it showed.

The various players in this unholy free-for-all included a divided Lebanese military consisting of nearly equal parts Christian and Muslim, various militia factions such as Hezbollah, or in English – the "Party of God," the Christian Phalanges (a mostly secular democratic political party supported by the Maronite Christian population), the Druze (a mystical offshoot of Islam), the Palestinian Liberation

Organization (PLO), and Syrian Occupation Forces. There were also occasional incursions by the Israeli Defense Forces, and peacekeeping forces of the United Nations, including the United States.

The Christian population of Lebanon, (most of which are a regional and ethnic subset of the Roman Catholic Church known as "Maronites" after a local patron Saint named "Maron"), experienced great influence in times past, when the French had colonial oversight of the country from 1920-43. In the early days of World War II, after France was invaded and occupied by Hitler's Germany, the French largely abandoned their stake in Lebanon and a dramatic power shift occurred. Lebanese independence was granted by the Free-French government, which was operating in exile under the leadership of Charles de Gaulle from London after 1940. The stability of Lebanon, and the Middle East in general, was no longer a top priority of the former colonial powers, particularly France and England, who were fighting against the Nazis for their very existence.

During World War II, the Allies managed to fend off the Nazis from Lebanon and British Palestine. In the redrawing of national boundaries after the Allied victory over Germany, Israel was granted official statehood in 1948. The level of enthusiasm among European Jews to repopulate their historic homeland in hopes of a safe haven was understandably high after the Nazi Holocaust. And yet, the Palestinian people who were displaced by these developments were understandably provoked, as were their Arab neighbors.

Boatloads of Jewish people arriving from all over the world to resettle the newly created state of Israel led to Arab-Israeli wars in 1948 and 1967. These conflicts further uprooted Palestinians, many of whom had lost lands and homes to the creation of the new Jewish state. Previous talks about a two-state solution never materialized.

A consequent humanitarian crisis in the Middle East followed the armed conflicts of World War II and the 1948 declaration of Israel as a new nation set apart to be settled by Jewish refugees from war-torn Europe and elsewhere. It is estimated that one-hundred thousand Palestinian refugees came north into Lebanon during the years between 1948 and 1967.

By 1975, the amalgamation of all of these disparate and often competing elements – a divided Lebanon along Christian and Islamic fault lines, the Syrians, the Israelis, and the clash of various sectarian militias like Hezbollah and the Christian Phalangists had concocted a nasty brew of chronic magnitude. Adding to this smoldering powder-keg of bellicosity, was the encroaching overlay of the Cold War between the US and the Soviet Union that was being played out all over the world from Korea, Southeast Asia, many places on the African continent, Central and South America, Cuba, and along both sides of the Iron Curtain in Europe - east and west. It was a fact that the bigger stake of the Lebanese Civil War was its undeniable emergence as a proxy battlefield between the remaining post-World War II superpowers and their competing ideologies – specifically a democratic and free America spreading individual freedoms and democracy versus the Union of Soviet Socialist Republics and their vision of state-run communism throughout the world.

Leftist militias, pan-Arabic groups, Syria, and Islamic terror groups like Hezbollah, were armed and supported by the Soviets; while the Christian militias and the Israelis were firmly backed by the United States of America. It was truly a mess by the mid-80s when the USS *Saratoga*, and her battle group, was assigned to project American power and foreign policy in this contested region. It was the standing responsibility of the US Sixth Fleet to maintain maritime law and freedom in the Mediterranean Sea and to provide oversight and tactical aerial support in order to protect American interests in this volatile region.

In a matter of months, *Saratoga* would be the flag ship of the largest naval battle group to engage in combat operations since World War Two. Even before the Libyan conflict and the *Achille Lauro* incident, the *Saratoga* had been directed to respond to the slaying of a US Navy Petty Officer, Robert Stethem, in Beirut, Lebanon on June 15, 1985. Stethem was killed by Hezbollah terrorists who had hijacked the commercial aircraft upon which the young sailor was making his way home. Petty Officer Stethem, a young Navy underwater-construction diver, was singled out, tortured, killed, and his body dumped on the airport tarmac in Beirut, simply because he was carrying a U.S. passport and a military identification card.

Beyond a fellow sailor's tragic death, the geo-complexities that were the context of *Saratoga*'s Med/IO deployment in 1985-86 were far from the minds of most of us, at least for a few days, as we pulled into the port of Haifa, Israel for a welcome respite. Though the automatic weapons fire could still be heard in nearby Southern Lebanon, the *Saratoga*'s arrival to the port of Haifa garnered much more attention. The gunfire in Lebanon was a daily occurrence in 1985. It was not every day, however, that a large aircraft carrier like the *Saratoga* pulled into port. The USS *Saratoga* was 1,063 feet long with a keel forty feet below the water line. From the water level to the flight deck level was another seventy feet. And most impressively, the Saratoga had a crew and airwing of over 5,000 men with money in their pockets and a desire to spend it one way, or another.

We had already pulled into Toulon, France for our first Med/IO port visit in late September. Many sailors had been satisfied to stay close to port in the gritty French naval seaport-town of Toulon. There were enough bars, strip clubs, and restaurants to satisfy the majority. Others, like myself, filtered out to take advantage of the budget priced tours to Paris or Monaco set up by the Ship's Special Services Division for men of enlisted rank. Naval tradition had long established the strict separation of officers and enlisted men on board ships to lessen the chances of mutiny in the old days "*when ships were made of wood and men were made of steel*" as some say.

While commissioned officers having a college degree and an officer's commission, and the enlisted men and women of the Navy worked closely together in my era of military service, there were strict rules against social fraternization between these two classes of naval personnel. Other branches of the military operate similarly with regard to non-fraternization between officers and enlisted, but no branch of the military is as insistent as the Navy upon retaining its age-old sea-going traditions. The Navy is known, among the branches of the military, for its adherence to tradition.

In the 1980s, when I served, only men were assigned to combatant ships like the *Saratoga*. Then on November 30, 1993, President Bill Clinton repealed a prohibition against women serving on combat vessels. Prior to this reversal, women had served only on non-combatant ships, and in various positions on shore-based naval installations. In the same year, 1993, Bill Clinton softened the military's prohibition against homosexuality with the introduction of his "Don't Ask – Don't Tell" policy that required that homosexual military personnel keep their sexual orientation to themselves, yet they were from that time protected from the threat of being separated from the service because of their sexual orientation.

In 2010, President Barak Obama would overturn the "Don't Ask: Don't Tell" policy, which had been in place since 1993, to offer full military service opportunities to publicly self-avowed and practicing homosexual soldiers, sailors, airman, and marines. In 2010,

Obama also authorized first steps to begin the integration of women into submarine, infantry, special operations, and air assault assignments. By 2016, Obama had ordered the Marine Corps to open all combat arms career fields to women. To date, few women have pursued the combat roles of infantry and special operations, and those few had mixed reviews amid some operational complications. The Navy maintains that the integration of women on combatant ships and submarines has had general success with some social and operational complications that were likely expected, such as pregnancies before or during deployment.

The Marine Times reported on March 5, 2018 that only eleven women were serving in the infantry career fields, none had attempted the Basic Reconnaissance Course, and that there were no female snipers. The same conspicuous absence of women is noted among the US Navy Seals and the Army Special Forces; though a small number of women have successfully completed the grueling US Army Ranger School and received the coveted Ranger Tabs which are required, but not a guarantee, to serve "on-the-line" as combat infantry in the U.S. Army's elite 75th Ranger Regiment. Undoubtedly, over the past few decades, long standing Naval traditions have been tested, but the segregation of officers and enlisted personnel beyond their interaction on duty will likely remain.

Following our port visit to Toulon and the *Saratoga*'s involvement in the international incident surrounding the *Achille Lauro* high jacking from October 7-10, 1985, we pulled into Haifa for a highly anticipated port of call. Even to the religious cynics onboard the *Saratoga*, a port visit to the ancient land of Israel seemed to catch the imagination of many. Israel is the birthplace of the world's three major monotheistic religions: Judaism, Christianity, and Islam. The *Saratoga*'s Cruise Book recorded that 1,700 sailors and marines out of the 5,000 Ship's Company and Air Wing signed up to take one or more of the special Holy Land tours offered by the Ship's Special Services Division. Over a hundred of us had signed up for the chaplain's three day Holy Land Baptism Tour, and judging from the number of pictures of this excursion included in *Saratoga*'s 1985-86 Cruise Book, it was the most popular of the several excursions offered by the Ship's Services Division.

I was among a group of over one hundred sailors from the *Saratoga*, mostly between the ages of 19-24, who seized this opportunity to profess our personal faith in Jesus Christ through believer's baptism by being immersed in the Jordan River. I was 19, but this was not my first baptism. Having been raised in a church going Baptist family, my first baptismal experience at the age of seven had been, for me, no more than getting dunked. I've jokingly said that on my first baptism experience, I went in a dry devil and came out a wet devil. I really just went for a swim. While I had participated in a religious ritual, there had been no change in my life.

About eight years later, at the age of 16, I began a personal relationship with God through Jesus Christ as my Savior and Lord. That experience occurred while I was attending a summer church camp for teenagers in August of 1982. It would be a few more years, however, before this new spiritual seed would sprout more fully. The long deployment onboard the *Saratoga*, with its solace, deprivation, trials, and adventures turned out to be the perfect setting for my Christian walk to increase in depth and urgency. My second baptism experience, administered by the *Saratoga*'s Command Chaplain, Hugo Hammond, would symbolize my genuine personal encounter with Jesus Christ at the church camp just over two years earlier.

In the weeks and months that followed the baptism experience in the Jordan River, many of those baptized that day would have an apparent impact upon a growing number of crew-members onboard the *Saratoga* as the Christian movement gained momentum. Indeed, during that eventful eight-month tour of duty, the number impacted would increase over the months to come. Our return from the Chaplain's Baptism Tour marked the beginning of an authentic spiritual awakening movement that would result in a good number of the *Saratoga's* crew and airwing discovering, or rediscovering, the importance and personal fulfillment of a closer walk with Jesus Christ.

For me, the experience of my conversion to Christ had occurred at the age of 16, while attending a summer church camp for teenage students in 1982. My second baptismal experience, administered by the *Saratoga's* Command Chaplain, Hugo Hammond, symbolized the real, life-changing encounter with Jesus Christ which I had experienced at the church camp just over two years previously.

Making a public profession of faith through baptism has long been central to Christian identity because of Jesus' words instructing his followers to "Go and make disciples of all the nations, baptizing them in the name of the Father, the Son, and the Holy Spirit; and teaching them to obey everything I have taught you. And I will be with you to the end of the age."[3] Scripture records that Jesus himself was baptized in the Jordan River by a prominent, yet controversial, spiritual ascetic named John the Baptist.

In short, baptism is a beautiful symbol that expresses one's personal faith in and identification with Jesus Christ's death, burial, and resurrection.[4] The believer has died to their old way of life dominated by self and sin (symbolized by immersion into the water) and is now raised to walk in a new way of life (symbolized by emerging from the water).

In fact, when addressing the subject of baptism, Scripture always states that baptism follows belief. As a pastor, I have said many times before baptizing new believers, that baptism, itself, doesn't save you. The baptism experience is simply a public profession of the belief, or faith, of the one being baptized, but does not, in and of itself, guarantee their salvation. Baptism is, however, an important symbol expressing one's salvation, as well as an act of obedience to the Lord's command to be baptized. In summary, however, baptism is an outward expression of an inward experience.

The Baptismal Certificate issued by the *Saratoga's* chaplains office reads: "Thomas Garrison Ferrell was baptized in the Jordon River on 9 November 1985 during the Mediterranean-Indian Ocean Deployment of the USS Saratoga (CV-60). This baptism was provided upon his profession of faith and was administered in the name of the Father and the Son and the Holy Spirit."

The certificate, with an image of the Saratoga in the graphic design, was signed by H.S. Hammond, Command Chaplain, and a witness, whose name is difficult to read. As I noted above the growing religious fervor on our ship, resulted in over a hundred of us being baptized during our three-day tour which was arranged by the chaplain's office! The *Saratoga's* 1985-86 cruise book includes a picture of a large group of young sailors on the banks of the Jordan River singing with smiling faces, and some with hand upstretched towards heaven. Waiting our turn, we were on the riverbank watching our brothers in Christ with arms crossed over their chests, like dead men, leaning back under the firm grasp of Chaplain Hammond. Each one, at his turn, acknowledged Jesus as Lord. Then, in "trust-fall fashion," each fell back effortlessly into the water, before coming forth from this historic stream, as men who were resurrected to walk in a new way of life.

CHAPTER 2

IT'S NOT JUST A JOB: IT'S AN ADVENTURE!

By the time I was baptized in the Jordan River, roughly two months into our eight-month deployment, it had already been an eventful cruise. Just before our port call to Haifa, Israel, the *Saratoga* made international news following the apprehension of the terrorist cell on 10 October 1985. National news covered the story of F-14s from the *Saratoga* intercepting the hijackers which belonged to a Terrorist Group known as The Palestinian Liberation Front, or PLF. The story was being carried across the country on the front page of daily papers like the LA *Times* and the *New York Times*. I should add that in the mid-80s, before the internet and long before social media, those who were deployed were more likely to be in the dark regarding public awareness and perception back on the home front.

Apart from the snail mail that typically arrived every week on a Grumman C-2 Greyhound, referred to by sailors and marines as a COD (Carrier On-Board Delivery), we actually had little contact with the outside world. Working in CIC, with the minimum of a Secret Clearance, OS's generally knew a good bit about the operational details of the missions and maneuvers with which we were directly involved. Beyond that; the Military mandate of "Need to Know" governed the distribution of all classified information, and we were occasionally reminded of everyone's favorite Navy proverb that we had been taught in Boot Camp: "Loose Lips Sink Ships." I think this navy proverb was a favorite simply because it is nearly impossible to forget. I have even heard drunk sailors proudly recite it with respectable accuracy as they waited in queue for the liberty boats that ferried us back and forth to the *Saratoga* after a long day and night in port. Admittedly; it sounds a bit ridiculous when badly slurred. But it seemed that everyone could remember that one. Surprisingly, I still remember it well after thirty-two years! "Loooosh Lipppssss Shhhinkkk Shipppppsssssss!" An index finger placed over the lips of the one badly slurring the proverb makes it all the more comical.

Typically, most of the crewmembers on a Navy ship have a pretty limited scope of awareness regarding the operational and tactical details beyond their particular duty assignment. You can imagine that cooks, for example, then formally known as Mess Specialists (or informally as Soup Burners), Hospital Corpsmen (with the unfortunate informal name of "Pecker Checkers," rumored as such due to incidents of sexually transmitted diseases in the navy), Hull Technicians ("Turd Chasers" due to their welding skills they were invariably tasked with plumbing repairs (any further explanation seems unnecessary), and Boatswain's Mates ("Deck Apes") because they were forever jumping around tying things down and were known to be rather messy due to their work environment. These important ratings were naturally less situationally aware of the ship's operations than were Operations Specialists, who were known as "Scope Dopes," because we were always looking for bad guys on our radar screens.

This is not to assert that one rating is superior to another in terms of its actual usefulness onboard ship. When it gets right down to the nitty gritty; some of the less vainglorious occupations might actually be the most esteemed, in some respects, onboard a ship. I remember being counseled upon arrival to the *Saratoga* that there were three people (ratings) that I did not want to... well...let's just say that I should be careful not to upset them. They are: Mess Specialists who cook the food, Hospital Corpsmen who maintain the shot records, and Disbursing Clerks who administer the paychecks. These particular folks, if not treated with due respect, could spit in your food, lose your shot records, and mess with your pay. When you start talking about food, money, and pain, it becomes obvious that the personnel in these three vocational ratings could hit you where it really counts.

Yet, still, on the floating city that is an aircraft carrier, most people were caught up in simply doing their jobs, staying in the good graces of their immediate superiors, and thinking about an eventual return home. That being the case, it is a fact that limited and segmented knowledge with regard to one's occupational scope of concern drove the day to day rhythms on an aircraft carrier. Most days were just like the previous day. I remember going without seeing land for thirty consecutive days three different times in that eight-month deployment. On such prolonged periods at sea; I recall that each member of the crew was rationed a few beers on a "Steel Beach Day" held up on the Flight Deck as Flight Ops were curtailed. We had volleyball games, roller skating, jogging, lying around in the sun, Frisbee and football tossing; and the dispensation of two, or was it three, beers each. Actually, the beer distribution was probably just an old Navy trick to prevent outright mutiny among the crew during such extended periods at sea. But it warmed my heart to see how well I was treated by my shipmates in the days leading up to "the Steel Beach Party." Perhaps, it was because I was known in OI Division as a teetotaler and there were, apparently, high hopes among my shipmates to see who might secure my ration of grog for himself!

Generally, while at sea, I passed most of my free time, when I wasn't working in CIC, by sleeping, eating, reading the Bible, lifting weights, and I even managed to take two college courses (English Composition 101 & General Psychology) through the Navy's PACE Program (Program for Afloat College Education). We actually had a few college professors onboard during our deployment to offer these classes in person before the advent of distance learning. Writing letters to loved ones back home and reading and rereading their replies was also a common pastime of lonely sailors far off at sea. In addition to her prayers, my mother was consistent and faithful in sending care packages with lots of good things to eat. One of the things she sent that I recall enjoying most, was the fan mail I received from her second-grade students at Clear Creek Elementary School, just southeast of Charlotte. Comical stick figures colored over with Crayola crayons and side-splitting captions could soften the heart of a devil. I often shared these drawings with my shipmates just to test my thesis.

I will say that being an OS on a ship was nice for several reasons. With the exception of standing watch as a lookout, you generally worked in an airconditioned space, which was necessary to keep the NTDS (Naval Tactical Data System) up and running properly. In the mid-1980s, the NTDS was, in fact, the forerunner to the internet. Through this data link shared by various ships, each ship's limited radar picture was extended in cooperation with the other ships' radar pictures so that we had, displayed on the screen of the NTDS console, a real time image of the surface contacts potentially within a five hundred-mile range. The same was true for the air picture. OS's were also aware of the operational details such as the ship's exact location, the location and type of other vessels in the area, the presence or absence of adversarial submarines, and the vector and general destination of the combat air patrols (CAPs) that had been launched from one of the four steam-driven catapults on the flight deck.

What I really appreciated was the privilege I had to know where we were at any given time. Since it was the Captain's space and his General Quarters Station, you would never go up to the bridge unless you were on that watch station at the moment. But, as an OS, you could walk into Combat Information Center at any hour of the day and check out the charts, radar picture, plot boards, classified cables, and pour through the many volumes of *Jane's Fighting Ships* that contained information on the various navies around the world; both friend and foe.

Jane's listed the silhouettes, specifications, weaponry platforms, strengths and weaknesses, crew size, and other information for all of the military ships and airplanes that we might encounter. For most of the rest of the crew and airwing; these were things to which they did not have access. Were we near the coast? In what country are those twinkling lights on the shoreline located? How deep is the water here? How fast are we going? What is our max speed? Are there any Soviet ships tailing us beyond the horizon right now? Stuff like that we always knew, or at least we could ask about without being chastised for being too nosy or, worse yet, being suspected of international intrigue.

But, to give our Captain, Jerry Unruh, his due as the thoughtful leader that he was, I will say, when it came to the big operations like the interception of terrorists by *Saratoga*'s fighter jets, our entire crew was kept reasonably abreast of what was going on. The Captain and the Executive Officer came on closed circuit television just prior to the interception and apprehension of the terrorists and informed the crew that we were ordered from higher command to apprehend terrorists and we would all be hearing more about the details soon. Captain Unruh, who had been a fighter pilot in Viet Nam and also served as the Commanding Officer of the famed TOP GUN School before coming to *Saratoga*, projected a calm confidence on the closed-circuit address to the entire crew and he affirmed the importance of our entire crew pulling together to ensure that the upcoming mission was a success.

This brief live video announcement by the Captain was broadcast to the *Saratoga's* Crew shortly after the events of the hijacking of the *Achille Lauro* had occurred, and just as the response of the *Saratoga* was about to unfold. Undoubtedly, this effort by the Commanding Officer made the entire crew feel as if we were part of something important. And we were! As the African proverb states that it takes a village to raise a child, so it takes the efforts of the entire crew and airwing to fulfill the responsibilities of a deployed aircraft carrier.

As Captain Unruh gave his crew a brief basic overview of the situation, and its importance to our national security, his words were punctuated with a phrase similar to what we had been taught in firefighting training back in boot camp. In Navy Boot Camp; everybody is trained in firefighting because of the immense danger of shipboard fires in battle as well as in normal steaming conditions. If, and when, a ship catches fire; there is no Fire Department, beyond the crew itself, upon which you can call. In stiff newly issued Navy dungarees, having donned fire suits with visor-helmets, Boot Camp recruits approach blazing fires in training with active water hoses. The mantra we were taught to shout in unison while approaching the blaze was: "Let's go get it!" But, this time, in the case of the Skipper's call to arms, the firefighting mantra was modified to; "Let's go get 'em!" You can bet the crew was motivated by being let in on these operational details by their Captain; whose communication was always personable and spirited. In retrospect; I believe that we would have followed Captain Unruh and the leadership of the *Saratoga* to the gates of Hell with water pistols. Now, granted, I may be in slight danger of embellishment after all of these years. But I really think we would have.

Shortly after the captain's communication with the crew via closed circuit television, the *Saratoga* took part in the "flashpoint" operation of intercepting the terrorist high-jackers. The dictionary defines flashpoint as "a critical situation or *area (italics mine)* having the potential of erupting into sudden violence." The Middle East is the "poster child" for flashpoints as it has been for thousands of years. Indeed, looming shadows of potential conflict are in the news even as I write these words. The potential for armed conflict is as real today as it was when I served. Differing worldviews and agendas are at play for supremacy in our day and time; and they will always be. America, China, Russia, Iran, and North Korea, are but a few of the most notable nation states throwing elbows on the world stage today. Beyond these national rivalries, Islamic terrorism has proven to be a frequent cause of conflict in various flashpoints around the world.

The Saratoga engaged in several flashpoint operations; not the least of which was the *Achille Lauro* operation. The logbook of the

Achille Lauro records how the forty-year old Italian Cruise Ship had pulled out of Genoa, Italy on October 7, 1985 with a 12-day cruise of the Mediterranean Sea making up her itinerary. Aboard the *Achille Lauro* were 748 passengers, including nearly a dozen American citizens, in addition to the ship's crew of several hundred employees. Later that day, on October 7, the *Achille Lauro* docked at Alexandria, Egypt where 651 passengers disembarked to tour the Pyramids with plans to rendezvous with the ship later at Port Said, Egypt. After the sightseers departed, four heavily armed Palestinian gunmen with AK-47s took control of the ship, dismissed the captain, forcibly hijacked the ship, and demanded the ship to sail for Tartus, Syria. The terrorists also demanded the release of fifty fellow Palestinian terrorists imprisoned by the Israeli government. Israel, of course, refused to comply with the terrorist's demands.

The crew and remaining 97 passengers would experience a nightmare of terror as the ship sailed to Tartus. Under pressure from both the Italian and American governments the Syrian government denied the ship entry, refusing to allow it to tie up to the dock at Tartus. In growing frustration, members of the PLF shot and killed Leon Klinghoffer, an elderly Jewish-American man confined to a wheelchair, at approximately 3:00 pm on October 8. Then, the terrorists forced a Portuguese waiter in the cruise ship's company to push Mr. Klinghoffer's lifeless body overboard. Klinghoffer was undoubtedly singled out because of his American passport, his Jewish name, and his religious heritage. After Klinghoffer's execution, the hijackers steered the ship to the nearby island of Cyprus, where they were also denied port entry.

By this time, Yasser Arafat, the controversial but widely known leader of the Palestinian Liberation Organization (PLO), had become involved in the negotiations. Arafat directed Muhammed Zaidan, also known as Abu Abbas, the leader of the PLF, to proceed to Cairo in order to mediate the situation. Frustrated by the denial of entry to Cyprus, the hijackers demanded a commercial jetliner with safe passage to Tunisia. An Egyptian Boeing 737 commercial jetliner and crew was made available to the terrorists by the Egyptian government.

According to statements by the Egyptian Government, Zaidan had assured them that there had been no casualties in the seizure of the *Achille Lauro*. Zaidan began negotiations with Egypt to achieve entry of the ship back to Port Said and he demanded immunity from prosecution for the PLF hijackers. Shortly after the arrival of the *Achille Lauro*, the Egyptian government announced that the hijackers had disappeared upon arrival to Port Said and that their whereabouts were unknown. Shortly thereafter, the US received intelligence that the hijackers had boarded an Egyptian airliner bound for Tunisia. It was about that time that President Ronald Reagan decided to direct the *Saratoga* to intervene with aerial interception and redirection of the commandeered jetliner.

On October 10 four F-14s from the squadron VF-74 were launched from the *Saratoga* to intercept the Egyptian jetliner. Fighter-jets from VF-103 were vectored on a tangential support mission as well. These F-14 fighter jets were scrambled just twenty minutes after the *Saratoga* was given the green light to intercept the terrorists. These capable planes would be on station intercepting the jetliner within one hour and a half. Naval command and control communicated to the Captain of the commercial jetliner the necessity of landing the commandeered aircraft on a joint NATO base in Sigonilla, Sicily just as F-14s became visible alongside his Tunisian-bound jetliner.

The startled Egyptian commercial pilots complied with the U.S. Navy's command for them to set a course immediately for the NATO Base at Sigonilla, Sicily. Seal Team Six had been deployed to Naval Air Station Sigonilla to board the commandeered jetliner and, if necessary, to kill or capture Abu Abbas and the members of his terrorist cell. As is common, the Special Operations component of the mission to capture the terrorists has been kept in relative secrecy. Declassified CIA documents reveal that the Seals were immediately met with political and operational resistance from the Italian Government and, in particular, the "Carabinieri," which is the domestic law enforcement agency of Italy.[5]

Shortly after landing, the terrorists surrendered to the Carabinieri, who were, along with the SEALS, on hand for the apprehension. Undoubtedly, the terrorists preferred the option of surrendering to the Italians as opposed to the welcoming party from Navy Seal Team Six. Given the possibilities, the terrorists should count themselves fortunate. Little detail is given, but it is clear that the American government, not to mention the Seals, themselves, were less than enthusiastic about standing down to allow the Italians to make the arrest in this prickly diplomatic situation. But at the end of the day, the passengers of the *Achille Lauro* had been freed and the terrorists had been brought to justice; or so it seemed.

In a press briefing from the White House on October 11, 1985, President Reagan explained a bandage on his nose as treatment for skin cancer before launching into a brief summary of the operational details of the apprehension of the PLF terrorists. He stated his pride, and the pride of the nation, in the members of the military and intelligence community who participated in the apprehension of the terrorists. The president spoke of the *Saratoga*'s "flawless performance." In his closing remarks, the Commander in Chief stated: "These young Americans sent a message to terrorists everywhere; that is that you can run but you cannot hide."

In spite of the widespread positive press coverage immediately following the incident, President Reagan appeared to be on the defensive as he addressed the media in the Press Room. In fact, he had appeared somewhat rattled and unsure what to do about the situation when questioned on one news coverage broadcast before the interception of the jetliner was ordered. At that point, the story of the hijacking of the *Achille Lauro* was already being followed in the media. Leon Klinghoffer's death, however, was still an unknown part of the story due to the outright lies of the terrorists in their preliminary negotiations. The troubling discovery of Klinghoffer's death was, of course, a game changer, as well as a complicating revelation.

The hijacking was another example of the Cold War rivals, the United States and the Soviet Union, backing opposite sides in the volatile Middle East. On the one hand you had the Palestinians, supported by the Soviet Union, who demanded that Israel vacate the land they had recently occupied. And on the other hand, there were the American-backed Israelis, who had suffered six million casualties in a genocide attempt by Nazi Germany by Nazi Germany and who were intent upon keeping their ancestral lands recently reacquired. The specter of another "hot war" between the Israelis and Palestinians and their Arab allies always looms large in the Middle East.

Given the intensity of the Israeli-Palestinian Conflict, it was no surprise that not everyone was happy about the actions taken by the *Saratoga*. An LA *Times* article dated October 16, 1985 records that Egyptian President Hosni Mubarak demanded a public apology from the U.S. for forcing the Egyptian airliner carrying the PLF cell to land in Italy. To that audacious demand, President Reagan responded with one word, "Never!" The LA *Times* Staff Writer opined: "this blunt reply, uttered sternly...seemed certain to aggravate an already serious setback in U.S. relations with both Egypt and Italy."[6] Reagan even sent a "conciliatory letter" to Mubarak and declined to criticize him publicly; even though the Egyptian President had declared the actions of the US Navy "an act of piracy."

Mubarak wanted the terrorists to be set free with no consequences whatsoever, reasoning that the remaining passengers of the *Achille Lauro* had been released without further harm. He essentially wanted Leon Klinghoffer's death at the hands of the terrorists to go unpunished. Whether or not those were President Mubarak's personal views is less than certain. It is highly likely that Egypt's president was advocating an untenable request of immunity for the terrorists in response to immense pressure he was receiving from the radical Islamist elements within Egypt and the surrounding region. Their hatred for Israel and America was growing by the day.

In the end, the Italian government allowed Zaiden (Abu Abbas) to leave on bail; which he jumped and remained at large for nearly twenty years. In 1986, the four hijackers, ranging in age from 17-23, were tried in Italy along with eleven other PLF accomplices. Nine of these, including Zaiden, were tried in absentia. The three eldest high jackers received sentences ranging from 15-30 years in prison. During this time, it was confirmed by Israeli Intelligence Services that Zaiden had actually directed the hijacking via radio; and he later admitted as much. Zaiden was later apprehended in Iraq by US Forces in 2003, where he was held for suspicion as an enemy combatant. He would die in American custody one year later.

The interception of the *Achille Lauro* high jackers would not be the last time in its 1985-86 Med/IO Deployment that the USS *Saratoga* would be called into action. Unbeknownst to us at the time of our Haifa port of call in October, our scheduled six-month Med Cruise would soon be extended for two extra months and our assignment would also include time in the Indian Ocean. We would, in fact, become the tip of the spear in a three-carrier battle group directed to engage the Libyan Navy which was backed and armed by our chief global adversary; the Soviet Union.

The Soviet Fleet would be an ever-present threat on that cruise, which was arguably, in retrospect, the apex of the Cold War. In just a few short years after our return from these confrontations with our Cold War adversary, the Soviet Union would cease to exist, and many of the Warsaw Pact nations that were its vassal states would achieve their independence. Little did we expect, on that cloudless day being baptized in the Jordan River, that we would soon be a part of the largest armada assembled for a sea battle since World War II.

On March 23, 1986, Soviet-constructed naval vessels procured by the Libyan Navy and flying the Libyan flag would fire aggressively upon aircraft of our battle group. Consequently, we counterattacked with the air assets of the *Saratoga* as well as with U.S. Navy surface vessels in our battle group. Three Soviet-made "Nanuchka" Class Corvettes armed with Guided Missiles under Libyan flag would be destroyed in the Gulf of Sidra. Several shore-based Libyan radar installations would also be hit by air-born U.S. naval munitions. The Libyan death count would be conservatively numbered in the high twenties. It is very possible that Soviet military advisors were also among the dead. Between these two incidents--the *Achille Lauro* hijacking and the Libyan "Line of Death" operations in the Gulf of Sidra, the *Saratoga* had demonstrated that the United States was moving in a new direction, characterized by determination and resolve. I am convinced that these two events, in their time period (1985-86), contributed significantly to a major turning point in our nation's morale and patriotism.

CHAPTER 3
DEAD IN THE WATER

As newly minted sailors straight out of boot camp in the late summer of 1984, we were stepping onto the streets of a nation with mixed feelings about the military, to put it mildly. Post-Vietnam anti-military sentiment lingered, and the U.S. military had been on a long "losing streak," ever since achieving an unprecedented victory of global size and scope in 1945 with the conclusion of World War II. During that war, from 1941-45, the American people largely pulled together to support the war effort to beat the Nazis in Europe and their allies, the Japanese, in the Pacific Theater.

Yet this American solidarity, so evident from 1941-45, followed a long period of isolationism and indifference towards any more military engagements after the carnage of World War I. From 1917-1919, American service members fought alongside their European allies against a strong and newly unified industrial and militarized Germany. In what was afterward called "the War to end all wars," American casualties in World War I mounted to 116,708 dead and over 204,000 wounded during the two years that the U.S. was engaged in the European conflict. The horrid conditions of extended trench warfare and the inception of modern artillery, heavy weapons, and even chemical nerve agents, such as mustard gas, ensured that the American population would be reluctant to enter into any military conflict again, at least for the foreseeable future.

Through the late 1930s, Americans kept their attention focused at home as the German Army under Adolph Hitler invaded and occupied Poland and France in 1939.[7] German aggression, as evident as it was by 1939, seemed far away and many Americans didn't want to be involved in another European War. But Hitler's ambition knew no bounds and Germany added Italy and Japan as allies to their cause in September 27, 1940 with the Tripartite Pact, also known as the Axis Alliance. Japan's aggression in the Pacific region took a giant leap forward with their stealth bombing attack on U.S. Naval Forces at Pearl Harbor, Hawaii on December 7, 1941. The American public was incensed, and President Franklin D. Roosevelt rallied the nation with the retaliatory cry, "Remember Pearl Harbor!" Military recruiting stations appeared, and young men left their civilian occupations to go to fight the Germans and the Japanese. Women also volunteered for military service opportunities, and they often filled vacant civilian job openings previously occupied by men, who were suddenly away fighting the war.

Americans planted victory gardens, willfully accepted food and gas ration cards, and recycled rubber and scrap metal to support the boys overseas fighting for our freedom. I have a large wooden plaque dated 1944, from the War Production Board, acknowledging Billy Ferrell, my dad, as a Junior Commando in the Civilian Army of the U.S.A. At the age of ten, Dad was pulling his little red wagon around the streets of his 4th Ward apartment home in Charlotte, North Carolina and he won a scrap metal collection contest for doing so. As a prize, Dad got a flight in a small private airplane and a plaque signed by the

Governor of North Carolina, J. Melville Broughton. I can tell you that plaque was proudly hung by my Dad in our storage shed all during my growing up years until our home was sold many years later.

The sustained solidarity of the American people in support of the military in World War II set a standard that would prove impossible to match in the decades that followed. Unfortunately, in those same decades, we would face an adversary every bit as driven and dangerous as the Axis Powers we had defeated in World War—the Soviet Union. Yet, the Soviet Union had joined on with our team of allies against the Germans and Japanese, only after Hitler had ambitiously invaded Russia on June 22, 1941. Prior to this development, Nazi Germany and the USSR had been allies, even participating together in the invasion of Poland in 1939. But the Soviets changed sides after Hitler's sudden betrayal of a previous mutual pact of alliance between the Nazis and the Soviet communists. The big leaders of the allied cause against the Nazis in World War II would become American President Franklin D. Roosevelt, Great Britain's Prime Minister Winston Churchill, and the General Secretary of the Communist Party of the Soviet Union Josef Stalin.

As a result of the wartime alliance between the U.S. and the Soviets, the American government was initially reluctant to oppose the Soviet Union's power grab of Eastern European nations in the days that followed the Allied defeat of Germany. This reluctance to counter the Soviet power grab of Eastern European nations formerly occupied by the Nazis was, in part, due to our alliance with the Soviet Union during World War Two. Hitler's invasion of the Soviet Union in 1941 had racked up massive death tolls among the Soviet people initially, but, as the months went by, the Soviets dug in to defend Moscow to the last person. Consequently, German casualties mounted, and the tide turned against them.

Before the tide turned in favor of the Soviets, the Axis Powers' force of almost three million men (considered the largest invasion force in military history) had captured five million Soviet Red Army troops and subjected them to the most horrible conditions imaginable. Hitler's attempt at genocide of the Soviet people, in order to provide "Lebensraum" or "breathing room" for German population and territorial expansion resulted in the death by starvation, and other causes, of over three million Soviet prisoners of war plus many more civilians as well.

The United States was reluctant to stem the tide of Soviet retribution and expansion following the defeat of the Axis powers. There were two basic reasons for this: 1) American post-war sympathy for what the Soviets had endured at the hands of the Germans, and (2) gratitude for the alliance with them which had broken the back of the Germans in a two-front war. As a result of American reluctance to intervene, the Eastern European countries that had recently been invaded and subjugated to Nazi power would, after the war, be liberated by the Allied powers only to be subjected to a fate similar to what they had experienced under the Nazis; and this time by the expansionist Soviet Union.

After the war, several other nations were assimilated into the Union of Soviet Socialist Republics (USSR). This "union" was dominated and controlled by Russia, and the "Republics" were that in name only. At its height, fifteen different "republics" made up the USSR.

This "union" had begun in 1922 after a bloody Russian Revolution. In the Russian Revolution, Vladimir Lenin, and an emergent Communist Party, harnessed the anger of millions of Russian serfs to overthrow the Romanov dynasty and centuries of Tsarist rule. Cumulative death tolls from the Russian revolution are estimated to be in the range of nine million to as high as fifty million, if deaths by starvation and deprivation are included. In fact, under the Soviet Communist dictatorship of Josef Stalin from 1924 until his death in 1953, twenty million people would die of torture, execution, and starvation as a result of Stalin's tyrannical means to maintain his hold on the Soviet Union.

The horrid details of Stalin's death camps, equal to, if not more lethal than Hitler's were well hidden from the world. Stalin even managed to charm American President Franklin D. Roosevelt, and an increasing number of elites in academia, entertainment, and within the Democratic party were enamored by the utopian claims of Communism. The revelation and extent of Stalin's brutality would later curb much of the public naivete about Communism.[8] Yet, American sympathy for Communism would resurface again in the 1960s among an array of left-leaning protest and civil rights groups who were attracted to some, or all, of the teachings of Karl Marx, Communism's founder.

In the *Communist Manifesto of* 1848, Marx and co-author Friedrich Engels, argued that human history was a series of conflicts over class warfare and the control of material property. Essentially, Marx urged the proletariat, or modern industrial working class, to overthrow their overlords (the business and propertied class) and to refashion society, and its means of production, into a State controlled entity. The State would oversee the management and the distribution of its production for use by the members of the Communist Party. With only one political party, and all of the social institutions under its control, freedom is inevitably limited, even squelched, due to the absolute necessity of the singular party in power using any means necessary to rid itself of any opposition to its control.

Yet, the ideals of equal outcomes and equal distribution as overseen by the Communist Party in a totalitarian state was the driving force of the Soviet gospel. In practical application, the ideal of equality gave way to "some being more equal than others." It is undeniable that state-run Communism always results in similar degrees of economic privation for most of the population; while a small group of party elites, relative to the whole of the population, enjoy material benefits that are not distributed to all. A recent article in the Miami Herald by Mario J. Penton dated January 04, 2019, has for its headline: *Grandson of Fidel Castro shares his life of luxury aboard yachts and more on Instagram.* While the communist rulers of Cuba live in luxury, the masses of people in communist Cuba are impoverished. This same scenario is repeated the world-over.

As Marx thought religion to be "the Opiate of the People," due to its attention to the hereafter, the traditional religion of Eastern Orthodox Christianity in the Soviet Union was coercively relegated to a minor position under state control. In effect, the Communist Party replaced the Church, and to many, Joseph Stalin took the place of God, or so it seemed.

By the early 1950s, the vast majority of the American people had an awareness of the stifling of freedoms in the USSR, as well as the extensive loss of lives perpetrated by the Soviet government against its own people. The fact that the Berlin Wall was built to keep East Germans within the communist-controlled portion of the city of Berlin, and not to keep West Berliners from leaving the democratic section of the city for the communist side made the situation fairly obvious to most. East Berlin was communist-controlled along with East Germany, while West Berlin and West Germany were free, democratic, and allied with the U.S. The term "Iron Curtain," describing the expansive boundaries of the Soviet Union, did not connote an image of desirability to those in the West who lived under the protections of free speech, a free press, and freedom of religion guaranteed in the first amendment of the U.S. Constitution.

That the Soviets had managed to achieve atomic weaponry and an appearance of military parity with the United States shortly after World War II is a testament to their prowess at espionage, which would become a shared hallmark between the two superpowers during the Cold War era. The tense standoff that was emerging with the Soviet Union would come to be known as the Cold War, precisely because it was not a "hot war," or a "shooting war," between the two superpowers themselves. Yet, no one can deny that an arms race of epic proportion between the USSR and the USA would characterize the decades after World War II, and until the disintegration of the Soviet Union in 1991. The fact that a nuclear-powered World War III never happened between the two adversaries is a testament to the benefits of armed deterrence.

In a nutshell, the Cold War was a four-decades long series of proxy shooting wars. United States military forces were deployed around the world with the goal of containing the spread of Communism while avoiding an outright full-scale war with the Soviets directly. The first conflict was a long stalemate in Korea in the early 1950s that ended in a draw. Both sides, communist North Korea and democratic South Korea agreed to a border along the 38th parallel to divide the countries. Then, after the Korean War, there was an even longer war in Vietnam.

There, the Communist North Vietnamese aggressively pushed south in a frenzied bid to possess the whole country as the North Koreans had attempted to do in their region. The American effort to aid the South Vietnamese government began in the early 1950s with the arrival of a relatively small number of U.S. military "advisors" to assist South Vietnamese forces. Troop numbers gradually increased, and the number of American forces directly involved in combat operations increased as well. By 1969, however, the US government was determined to begin a process of withdrawing its troops in this increasingly unpopular war.

In 1969, newly elected President Richard Nixon, who had promised to end the war in his presidential campaign, reversed the nearly two decades long build-up of troops with his "Vietnamization" policy. Nixon's policy gave the South Vietnamese gradual ownership of their civil war by reducing, over time, American troop levels.

In the post-World War II reality, a newly emergent Communist China began supplying, equipping, and reinforcing the emerging communist governments of North Korea and North Vietnam. In return, the Chinese gained political influence and used this newly acquired leverage to enhance its power within a growing sphere of influence. Having only recently arisen from its own bloody Communist Revolution in 1948, and propelled by its charismatic Communist revolutionary leader Mao Zedong, China was on the way to becoming a superpower itself. Yet, the Soviet Union was intent upon remaining the "elder-brother" in this growing fractious "family" of Communist states run by ruthless leaders. By the early 1950s, the Soviet Union, and China to a lesser degree, were both rising powers with whom the U.S. government hoped to avoid direct all-out warfare.

In the cases of Korea and Vietnam, the U.S. government applied only limited military force against the aggressive Communist incursions. The objective of this so-called "Containment Foreign Policy" was to limit the ideological and geographical spread of Communism through diplomacy, clandestine measures, and a cautious and measured application of military force. Some Americans were opposed to their government extending the military into these overseas conflicts to combat communist expansion. Other Americans felt that the civilian political leaders were misguided in their "limited- war" policy of containment, and that the American government was imposing too many limitations and rules of engagement upon its troops. By 1969, many Americans felt that the US was playing a losing game and the costs were being paid in American blood.

Yet, in spite of the United States strategy of limited engagement in proxy wars, many U.S. service members lost their lives in Korea and Vietnam. In Korea alone, 33,739 American lives were lost with 7,667 more unaccounted for. In Vietnam, 58,220 American service members were killed in action with another 1,589 reported missing in action.

Many Americans watched in dismay as the media covered the North Vietnamese marching into Saigon, the capital of South Viet Nam. The defining moment occurred when the last overloaded U.S. military helicopter lifted off of the U.S. embassy roof as the embassy staff and military rear guard lowered the U.S. Flag and abandoned the post. The symbolism of this evacuation was not lost on the American people, many of whom had grown to distrust their own government for various reasons.

Left behind were also many terrified South Vietnamese citizens who were begging to be taken aboard the overloaded aircraft. The sight of North Vietnamese troops shortly, thereafter, triumphantly looting their prize would haunt Americans forever. Even more haunting and enduring than that memory, will be the one of the nearly 60,000 Americans who gave their lives in a protracted war that seemed, in the end, to have made little difference.

By the time of the evacuation of the U.S. embassy in Saigon on April 30, 1975 and its seizure by the Communist forces of North Viet Nam, the American people had seen two wars of containment fought with only limited engagement. And the costs, in terms of human lives lost, had been painfully high. The cost in terms of the loss public faith in the government would be difficult to quantify, but this consequence would be a major factor in the declining morale and strained patriotism that would characterize our nation at least until the mid-80s. In addition to the downward spiral of the tragic loss in the Vietnam War, the Watergate scandal engulfing the Nixon presidency further soured the public trust from 1972-74, and thereafter.

By incessant media coverage, the American people were informed daily that the Nixon administration had orchestrated a break-in of the Democratic party headquarters in the Watergate Hotel in Washington, D.C. for the purpose of clandestine eavesdropping. Worse, yet, it was discovered through the tape-recorded conversations routinely kept by Nixon that he, himself, had tried to cover up the crime. Facing the certain possibility of a congressional impeachment trial, Richard Nixon resigned as President of the United States on August 9, 1974. This Watergate scandal only added to the national distrust of government that had intensified during the years of the Viet Nam War.

Consequently, by the mid-1970s, the very fabric of American patriotism had been torn asunder. The U.S. service members returning from Vietnam had come home to a nation that was at best divided in its support of them. This national mood of lethargy, introspection, and, for some, self-loathing would continue throughout the 1970s, and even through the mid-80s. But that would all change dramatically by the time the USS *Saratoga* returned from its celebrated eight-month Mediterranean/Indian Ocean deployment of 1985-86. I literally witnessed a changing of the mood and morale in our nation during those days in which I was privileged to serve my country. It was something to behold the new-found patriotism and positive media attention that greeted the *Saratoga*'s return from the Med/IO Cruise in April of 1986. That this support for the military has been so long sustained since that time is an even greater wonder, for which I am grateful.

CHAPTER 4

RED SKY IN THE MORNING

I reported to OS "A" School at Dam Neck Fleet Combat Training Center, near Virginia Beach, in mid-September 1984, just after graduation from boot camp at the Naval Recruit Training Command in Great Lakes, Illinois. Though I'm not sure about the rest of the country, anyone who served, or even lived, in the Tidewater area could testify that times were not good for the military in those days. The greater Norfolk area was reported to have the largest naval base in the world and a very high concentration of active duty military of the various branches serving on a great number of ships, bases, and naval air stations. In short, it seemed that a considerable percentage of the civilian population resented the military and these feelings of resentment were often evident. Because OS's in "A" School had to wear our uniforms everywhere we went on or off of the base; we were easily identified as sailors and sometimes harassed.

OS "A" School was strict, and it was, in some ways, like a redo of boot camp that lasted an additional seventeen weeks. In order to pass the regular scrutiny of our class Instructors and their frequent inspections, we had short, "Marine Corps-like" haircuts. We marched to class and then back to the barracks where we lived pretty much as we had in boot camp; except that we had a bit more freedom to eat candy and junk food. Also, most guys hung pictures in their lockers of attractive women in various stages of undress. So, things were a bit relaxed as compared with boot camp, but not much.

Looking back on it, I am shocked that I put up with such a Spartan existence for so long. Nine weeks of boot camp followed by seventeen weeks of OS "A" School made for nearly a seven-month marathon of meager living. As an eighteen-year-old enlisted sailor with no other compelling prospects at hand, I suppose it was just something that I accepted as my chosen lot in life.

And just like in boot camp, we were not permitted to have civilian clothes in our possession. The penalty for offenders was something akin to what would happen to despicable service members who were convicted of espionage, or so it seemed. The OS "A" School command had strict rules against its sailors wearing, or even possessing, civilian clothing. We were only permitted to have Navy Issue uniforms and Navy Issue workout clothes in our barracks. That was it, and let me tell you, if you went into Virginia Beach in a Navy uniform in 1984-85, you could expect the possibility of slurs, insults, and stare downs. Fights between sailors and civilians were not uncommon. So, it didn't take long before we discovered clandestine strategies for the stowage and retention of civilian clothes.

I kept my precious few civilian garments (civvies) in a small locker that I rented in a bowling alley not too far off the base at Dam Neck Fleet Combat Training Center Atlantic (DAM NECK FCTCLANT). I even had a few classmates that would date, without discretion, women of any caliber available in order to have a place to store their civilian clothes in the lairs of these said women. My locker rental fee was not cheap, but it seemed worth it when I considered the alternatives. It makes me just a little bit sad to think about how meager our existence was, but that is just the way it was. And it seemed to go on forever.

Truthfully, after the Vietnam War, which officially ended in 1975, and well into the mid-80s, the military was not treated with much respect in our country. In fact, the tone of the Carter presidency in general, and the Iran hostage rescue debacle that occurred on April 24-25, 1980, in particular, may have brought the publics' favorability rating of the military to its lowest point ever. During Carter's presidency, the U.S. government was humiliated by the Islamic Republic of Iran, whose student activists stormed the US Embassy in Tehran on November 4, 1979, seizing U.S. Government property and holding 52 American diplomates hostage for 444 days.

After the prolonged losing streak of the Vietnam War, the nation's patriotic fabric was nearly rent in two by the Iranian hostage crisis. Those who were alive at the time, and attentive to such things, could never forget President Jimmy Carter's so-called "malaise" speech, which he gave on July 15, 1979. The larger context of Carter's speech was the downward trend in morale and patriotism that had been noticeably strained in the U.S. since the Vietnam war era.

In addition to foreign affairs there was a pressing domestic problem. All across the nation, long lines of cars waited for the opportunity to pump gas at service stations. This gas shortage was exacerbated by tensions in the Middle East coupled with American dependency upon these very Arab nations for oil. It was increasingly obvious that our nation's collective patience seemed to be running out, correlating with the short supply of gasoline.

The gasoline shortage and depletion of American patience and morale seemed to hit rock bottom during the 4th of July holiday and vacation season, when the President was to make his ill-fated "Malaise" speech. A torrential rain had all but brought the nation's patriotic celebrations in Washington, DC to a complete standstill on July 4, 1979. More disconcerting was the fact that President Carter did not show up to make the scheduled speech on our nation's birthday, as presidents were expected to do each year. Rumors began to circulate that the president had taken ill, but few knew that his ailments had more to do with morale than physical impediments.

After reading his 4th of July speech, soon before its scheduled delivery, the first Lady, Rosalyn Carter, had told the President that the speech was terrible. Carter admitted that he, himself, had found it boring. Beyond a shocking anecdote bemoaning a terrible recent incident where a pregnant woman had been violently attacked in a Los Angeles gas line, much of the speech was a vague and droning recitation of federal energy policy. Suffering jet lag from a previous trip, the President called his advisors early in the morning on the 4th of July from his nearby retreat at Camp David to cancel his speaking engagement. Carter's advisors were shocked that the President was now refusing to make the speech in nearby Washington, DC later that day. Naturally, the President's advisors worried about the media response, and the public's perception. Never before had a president of the United States cancelled a speech with no explanation given. Actually, in a recent book about the "Malaise Speech" entitled: *What the Heck Are You Up to Mr. President*," author Kevin Mattson, recounts that the President told his objecting advisors: "I just don't want to bullshit the American people."[9]

When Carter finally made a public address on July 15, 1979, it appeared that he had done a bit of self-evaluation as an American, and he intended to direct the country to do the same. Though the President never used the term "malaise" in his speech, at least one of two influential politicians coined the descriptive term. Either Massachusetts Senator Ted Kennedy (D) and California Governor Ronald Reagan (R), who were both eyeing Carter's job in the upcoming presidential election of 1980, coined the descriptive term, and it stuck. The actual title of Jimmy Carter's Speech was "Crisis of Confidence," and many found it unsettling to hear a sitting president offer such a stinging indictment of the nation's morale, especially since the negative description was of a nation under his leadership.

Others felt that President Carter was just being transparent about conditions that were beyond his control, when he said: "All of the legislation in the world can't fix what is wrong with America...It is a crisis of confidence. It is a crisis that strikes at the very heart and soul of our national will. The erosion of confidence in the future is threatening to destroy the social and the political fabric of America." In less than four months, however, things would get even worse for Jimmy Carter, and for America.

On Monday, the 4th of November 1979, a group of Iranian students stormed the US Embassy in Tehran, taking more than 60 American diplomats and embassy staff hostage. Carter had permitted Iran's deposed Shah, who had been expelled from his country, to come to America for cancer treatments, which infuriated the Iranian revolutionaries. The Shah had been a strong-armed, but pro-Western autocrat, who was *persona non grata* in the emerging Islamic Revolution of Iran. The fledgling Islamic Iranian government declared their opposition to American interests, especially its support of Israel. They also expressed their complete disdain for the secular values and permissiveness that characterized American society. The decline of American morale would sink to greater depths as the media gave daily updates of the American hostages' dire situation in Iran. Images of the hostages blindfolded and kept against their will as captives of the Islamic Republic of Iran filled the airwaves and further eroded American confidence.

Finally, on April 24, 1980, President Carter authorized Operation Eagle Claw in order to bring the hostages home and to put a stop to the negative daily news coverage rattling an already anxious American electorate. After all, 1980 was an important election year and Jimmy Carter hoped to be rewarded for his efforts with a second term in the White House. The State Department's website reflects upon those days noting: "The crisis dominated the headlines and news broadcasts and made the Administration look weak and ineffectual. Although patient diplomacy conducted by Deputy Secretary Warren Christopher eventually resolved the crisis, Carter's foreign policy team often seemed weak and vacillating." I'm pretty sure that former President Carter would like to see that summary stated differently; nevertheless, the description is an accurate reflection of things as they were perceived by many Americans of that time.

With the hostage crisis in its sixth month, and negotiations proving unfruitful toward their release, Carter ordered a military mission as a last-ditch attempt to save the hostages. The US Army's Delta Force was given the lead role. Delta Force, the US Army's elite counter-terrorist unit had recently been created in 1977 by US Army Special Forces Colonel Charlie Beckwith. To his credit, Beckwith had served honorably in the Korean War, and had developed additional skills while serving with the British SAS during the Viet Nam War.

Beckwith was born in Atlanta, Georgia on January 22, 1929 and lettered in football with the University of Georgia Bulldogs. He was drafted to play with the Green Bay Packers, but the Korean War had just begun, and Beckwith opted for an Army Green uniform instead. By the mid-1970s, after the Vietnam War, Beckwith had accrued a lifetime of special operations experience. His service in the

Green Berets and as a liaison with the elite British SAS (Special Air Service) during Vietnam put him in a unique position. Because of his vast experience and large network of contacts, Beckwith would be tasked by senior military leaders to create a new and innovative counterterrorism unit. With his dedication to the task, Charlie Beckwith managed to get his fledgling plan through the labyrinths of the Department of Defense to gain the necessary bureaucratic support. The next hurdle was to cobble together congressional support and budget approval. By the time the Iran hostage crisis occurred in November of 1979, Delta Force had just come into existence, and it seemed the perfect choice to lead a mission set upon rescuing the American hostages in Iran.

The mission to free the captured American hostages, codenamed Operation Eagle Claw, was a complicated two-day affair with multiple engagement locations and various military personnel from differing units and branches. Army Rangers were tasked with securing a remote desert airfield location, along with Navy transport helicopters and refueling aircraft from the USS Nimitz, as well as Special Operations helicopters maintained and operated by the U.S. Air Force. The coordination of these various military service branches with different command and control structures proved to be the fundamental liability of the effort to rescue the hostages and restore America's national honor.

Operation Eagle Claw, as devised by the Pentagon and the Carter Administration, was aborted mid-mission due to poor command and control coordination of the various aircraft elements that were operating in difficult sandstorm conditions. Fuel limitations due to less than accurate distance and time calculations along with unforeseen mechanical difficulties resulted in the mission being aborted by President Carter in consultation with his military advisors. The final results were devastating, and the mission was an abject failure. One helicopter and one transport aircraft had been destroyed; five more helicopters were abandoned and captured, and most disturbingly, eight U.S. servicemen were killed and four more were seriously injured.

In order to avoid such cataclysmic results from miscommunication among various military commands involved in special operations, the United States Special Operations Command (USSOCOM) would be established a few years later by Ronald Reagan, President Carter's successor. On April 16, 1987, during President Reagan's second term, USSOCOM Headquarters would be based at MacDill Air Force Base where coordination of the special operations elements of the various military branches could be integrated into a singular authoritative command structure. Avoiding another fiasco like Operation Eagle Claw was the motivating factor.

By the time of the Iran Hostage Rescue Debacle, as it came to be known, on April 24, 1980, many Americans were looking for a new leader; and a new direction in America. As Carter had summarized the mood in his "Malaise Speech," many in America were feeling just what he was describing. This sense of being adrift at sea would be the current that would carry Ronald Reagan, the former governor of California, into the White House. Reagan, broadly known for his ebullient optimism, had been a Hollywood actor in the early days of movies, before his gradual involvement in pro-American and Conservative Political Activism. Reagan's involvement in conservative politics came at a time when Hollywood was under newfound scrutiny for its leftward drift and Communist sympathies. Reagan's timely rise to prominence within conservative circles would put him in the California Governor's Manion and, ultimately, the White House itself.

Ronald Reagan was inaugurated as the 40th President of the United States of America on January 20, 1981. The mood in American began to shift, almost immediately. On January 21, 1981, 444 days after the Iran Hostage Crisis began and just hours after President Ronald Reagan delivered his initial inaugural address, the Islamic Republic of Iran moved decisively to free the American hostages after 444 days of captivity during the one-term Carter presidency. Many historians believe firmly that the Iran Hostage Crisis, and its mishandling, prevented Jimmy Carter from achieving a second term as president.

Nearly four years after Reagan's inauguration on January 21, 1981, when I reported to the *Saratoga* at Naval Station Mayport, Florida in Mid-March of 1985; it seemed that the morale in America, and on the *Saratoga*, still left much to be desired. When I reported onboard the ship and began to familiarize myself with the general area, I was welcomed by some folks, both crewmembers and civilian shopkeepers, to the "Sorry Sara!" I quickly learned that this sad nickname had been in fairly common usage since the Viet-Nam War era. Her sister ship, the USS *Forrestal* (CV-59) was un-affectionately known at the "Forrest-Fire," after an infamous flight deck tragedy of 29 July 1967. An electrical anomaly on the *Forrestal* caused a Zuni rocket on an F-4B Phantom Fighter Jet to fire, striking the external fuel tank of an A-4 Skyhawk parked nearby on *Forrestal*'s flight deck. 134 sailors were killed and 161 more were injured in the conflagration that followed. One of the most well-known among the injured list was the late Arizona Senator John McCain.

The fire on the *Forrestal* was one more tragedy in a long line of unfortunate political incidents including the assassinations of John F. Kennedy and Martin Luther King Jr., the Vietnam War, divisive protests against the Vietnam war, the Watergate political scandal and subsequent resignation of President Richard Nixon, the evacuation of the US Embassy in Saigon in 1975, and the Iran Hostage Crisis of 1979-80. Years later, the *Forrestal* continued to be known as the "Forrest-fire," while the *Saratoga* would see its negative nickname "Sorry Sara" give way to the moniker "Super Sara" after the 1985-86 Med/IO cruise. Though the nickname "Super Sara" had been coined nearly two decades prior, it did not seem to stick until after her 1985-86 deployment.

An Associated Press article on November 11, 1985 was titled: "*Saratoga* Crew Hailed as Heroes in *Achille Lauro* High Jacking." The article reported on the euphoric response felt across the nation as the United States had experienced, a victory of sorts, over its adversaries. In the minds of many Americans, good had triumphed over evil. From Anchorage, Alaska where a newspaper published a half-page advertisement thanking the crew of the *Saratoga* to a hotel chain in Asheville, North Carolina that offered a free overnight stay to anyone on the crew of the *Saratoga*, Americans celebrated "good news" for a change. Notes of gratitude and celebration came addressed to the Captain from other nations including Great Britain, Australia, and West Germany.

It seems evident that these varied expressions of a more positive morale in the country correlated with the *Saratoga*'s involvement in the *Achille Lauro* high jacking. In fact, this welcome uptick in patriotism would continue on for years to come. In 1990, a three-hour made for TV movie "Voyage of Terror: The *Achille Lauro* Affair" starring Burt Lancaster (as Mr. Leon Klinghoffer) and Eva Marie Saint (as Mrs. Klinghoffer), based upon the *Achille Lauro* high jacking, was produced and aired. So it appears that within an eight-month period of time, in which the *Saratoga* was making headlines back in the States-- first with *Achille Lauro* then later with the Libyan "Line of Death" Operations, the nation finally began to see proof that America was on a new trajectory. The widely publicized accomplishments of the *Saratoga* gave tangible evidence to those looking for positive signs that America was back, at least militarily, from a long slump.

Danger Zone, a popular song recorded by Kenny Loggins in 1986, was one of the hit singles from the soundtrack to the immensely popular 1986 American motion picture *Top Gun*, revolving around NAVY F-14s and life on a super-carrier. Sailors returning from the *Saratoga*'s Med/IO Cruise sat in packed movie theaters along with other Americans and watched Tom Cruise catapulting off of the flight deck over a blue Mediterranean Sea. As these sailors had recently been witnesses to such events, they undoubtedly felt a fraternal connection to the drama on the screen and the greater sense of optimism sweeping our country. As I recall, the only time I ever wore my *Saratoga* Cruise Jacket was to see *Top Gun* while home on leave in Charlotte, North Carolina not many months after returning from the cruise. It is hard to overestimate the effect that the movie, and its musical soundtrack, had on the country.

Perhaps providentially, the accomplishments of Saratoga and the movie TOP GUN correlated, and even propelled, to affect an upward surge of American optimism at a time in which the Soviet Union was moving toward dissolution. In fact, the founder of the US Navy's TOP GUN program at Naval Air Station Miramar, California, quotes President Reagan's Secretary of the Navy, John Lehman, saying that the making of the movie TOP GUN, produced in 1985-86, "was designed with a particular audience in mind: the Russians."[10] What effect the movie had upon the Russians is open for debate, but there is no doubt that the movie became a favorite in America. According to Allmusic.com, the TOP GUN album soundtrack "remains a quintessential artifact of the mid-80s...and the album's hits still defined the bombastic melodramatic sound that dominated the pop charts of that era." The central lyric of *Danger Zone* promised: "Highway to the Danger Zone – I'll take you – Ridin' to the Danger Zone."

Call it providential timing, a feat of synchronized military and social engineering, luck, or just strange coincidence, but Reagan's leadership, the Saratoga's successful cruise, and the TOP GUN movie all seemed to coalesce into a game changing climate in America. Whatever you conclude, with the timing of the release of the movie *Top Gun*, and the return of *Saratoga* from its storied 85-86 cruise, Americans seemed to feel that our country had, indeed, gone to the Danger Zone; and for the first time in a long time, had come back with our heads held high. The tide had seemingly turned in America. The movie, an upsurge in military morale, and a telegenic President who garnered widespread respect were undeniable factors in a changing cultural climate in America.

And for a considerable number of us on the *Saratoga*, there was something even larger at play. The baptismal service in the Jordan River in October of 1985 had given illustration to something even greater that had occurred during months of a deployment punctuated by newsworthy successes that we would long remember.

CHAPTER 5
A SPIRITUAL POLLYWOG

My first baptismal experience had been in the baptistry of the First Baptist Church of Charlotte, North Carolina during a Sunday evening church service sometime in 1973, when I was seven years of age. Our Pastor, Dr. Carl E. Bates, had been President of the Southern Baptist Convention for two one-year terms in 1970-72. In the post- World War II "boom" years, the Southern Baptist Convention would become the largest Protestant denomination in the United States, and the largest Baptist body in the entire world. Southern Baptists, in keeping with their missionary heritage, were determined to spread the gospel of Jesus Christ and move from a regional body almost exclusively in the South to become a major player on the world's religious landscape.

In fact, Southern Baptists would reach their all-time high in recorded baptisms in the year 1972. That incredible number was 445,725 persons recorded as baptized in Southern Baptist churches in 1972. Whether or not Mark Twain's adage: "There are three kinds of lies: lies, damned lies, and statistics," applies to the Southern Baptist Convention's boast, only God knows. But, at least, Twain was honest enough to attribute the adage to Benjamin Disraeli. And I would hate to think that Mark Twain, an avowed skeptic, was more forthright and accountable than some of the churches who self-report their baptismal numbers to the Southern Baptist Convention.

Baptismal numbers aside, I was raised in a Southern Baptist family that typically attended the early service on Sunday morning at 8:00 am, followed by a Sunday School class for every age group - adults included - beginning at 9:30. Sunday School was invariably more interesting, to me, in those days than was the church service because you could play with friends and do many things so long as you were not caught. I also recall a very memorable experience constructing an "ark of the covenant," just like the one God told Moses to build so as to contain the Ten Commandments and several other sacred relics. The real Ark of the Covenant was so sacred that it was not to be touched frivolously by anyone upon penalty of death. I think Mr. Turner and Mr. Bailey, our Sunday School teachers in the fourth-grade boys' Sunday School class, decided to draw the line there on our simulation, obviously due to issues of liability.

Never mind that Moses' original Ark was constructed of exotic woods and precious metals and the like, while ours was made from a large cardboard box. I bet Moses and his helpers did not get to spray down their ark with numerous cans of spray paint (so many coats of brown paint were applied that I now wonder if our illustrious Sunday School teachers might have run out of lesson plans). At any rate, the experience was memorable, and our time spent spray painting the ark was fun. It was undoubtedly the first time I ever got high, but I digress.

Regarding my parents' compulsory church attendance, it is safe to say that I was attending church weekly – if not three times a week-- from nine months before I was born. My dad worked long hours at the First Union National Bank in downtown Charlotte. We called it "downtown Charlotte" back in the day, although now, the area around Charlotte's central intersection of Trade and Tryon Streets is commonly referred to as "Uptown." Through the clever efforts of a long running marketing campaign to boost the progressive image of Charlotte, also known as "the Queen City," Charlotte has since thrived and grown in size and influence. Two clear examples of Charlotte's progress were the acquisition of professional sports teams and its establishment as the Eastern headquarters of two major banks - Wells Fargo and Bank of America.

One surely contrived anecdote that captured the spirit of Charlotte in those days centered around the discovery of a classified Soviet list of fifty American cities and military bases that would be targeted for nuclear attack, if a conflict between the Cold War superpowers escalated to that point. The story relates that Charlotte was not on the Soviet "Hit List." Consequently, the people of Charlotte were highly offended and demanded a recount. Perhaps this sense of self-importance reflects the city's namesake, Queen Charlotte, the German born wife and consort of King George III, of England. King George III, of course, is infamous to Americans since he was the unhappy recipient of the Declaration of Independence in 1776. Mecklenburg County, which contains the city of Charlotte, is named after Queen Charlotte's birthplace in the Mecklenburg region of Northern Germany.

The majority of the early settlers of the Charlotte Mecklenburg area, however, were neither English nor German. Perhaps that is why the King insisted upon imposing his wife's name and birthplace upon the city and region. In fact, it was Scots-Irish settlers who made their way in considerable numbers to the Charlotte Mecklenburg area. These settlers migrated, in large part, south from Pennsylvania in the mid-1700s, as many of these 18th century immigrants had arrived from Ireland into the eastern seaport of Philadelphia. The Scots-Irish were scrappy, and religious, as a lot. The English had little use for their southern Scottish neighbors, abutting their northern border, who disliked the Catholic-like hierarchy and liturgy reflected in Anglicanism, the state church of England.

When a famine occurred in the Scottish borderland area in the mid-1600s, the English saw an opportunity to put these lowlander Scots to good use. The Crown sanctioned a plan for the relocation of the Southern Scots up to the Ulster region of Northern Ireland. The English Crown hoped that the Scots, once resettled to Northern Ireland, would be a buffer against the Roman Catholic Irish of the region. After all, Anglicans from England surely had more in common with Presbyterians from Southern Scotland than they did with Catholics in Northern Ireland, so the reasoning went. The English government also hoped this plan would create more "elbow room" and less conflict for the English citizens living near their northern border with Scotland. So away went large numbers of the Scots to the Ulster region of northern-Ireland.

Yet, things in Northern Ireland proved to be no better for these "Ulster Scots," as they became known. After about a hundred years living in conflict with the Catholic majority of Ulster, the struggle-hardened Ulster Scots would come in successive waves to have a try in the New World. Many came as indentured servants and nearly all, like most people of the time, were poor and out of necessity, industrious. My mother's family, the Garrisons, traced their heritage back to David Garrison, Sr, who migrated from Pennsylvania to the Mallard Creek section of Mecklenburg County in 1757. His land purchase would remain in the family until the 1970s, when it was sold by distant cousins to facilitate the expansion of the University of North Carolina at Charlotte.

Interestingly, a recent DNA test revealed my genetic heritage to be 81% Scottish/Irish/Welsh with 14% Balkan, almost 3% Iberian, 1.3% Italian, and 1.1% Native American. While some of these genetic trace elements are puzzling, it is fairly clear that the predominant branch in my family tree is the regional type known as "Scots-Irish," or "Scotch-Irish." It is highly likely that I, like many others from the Charlotte-Mecklenburg area specifically, and the nearby southern Appalachian region in general, am descended from the Ulster-Scots.

Cultural historians claim that a region's characteristics and values are reflected in the mindsets and worldview of its residents. Just like any other place, my hometown and region had its distinct peculiarities, even if they have grown fainter over time. For instance, many people know that Charlotte's NBA franchise, predominately owned by basketball legend and North Carolina native Michael Jordan, is named the Charlotte Hornets. Perhaps fewer people outside the area know that the British General Charles Cornwallis referred to the Charlotte-Mecklenburg area as a "Hornet's Nest" during the Revolutionary War. Oddly enough, General Cornwallis could rightly be credited with naming Charlotte's NBA franchise more than two hundred years before they came into existence! This claim to fame may be one of his more significant achievements that occurred before his death from a fever while serving the Crown in India and subsequent burial overlooking the Ganges River in 1805. Actually, Cornwallis was not short on accomplishments, but most of the people of the Charlotte Mecklenburg area were not at all fans of this British Officer in the pre-revolutionary days.

Mecklenburg County is known for declaring its independence from England even before the official Declaration of Independence, penned by Thomas Jefferson, was sent to King George III and his wife Queen Charlotte. Perhaps the rabble-rousing residents of Charlotte liked the name of their fair city; but not the queen for whom it was named. They certainly did not like the King for his exorbitant taxes and unsympathetic posture.

On Friday May 19, 1775, regional civilian militia leaders were meeting in the Charlotte courthouse at the intersection of Trade and Tryon Streets to discuss the exorbitant taxes imposed by England and the retaliatory blowback of the Boston Tea Party. As these militia leaders were meeting, they received word by a herald on horseback that British soldiers had fired upon colonialists at Lexington and Concord, in the Colony of Massachusetts. These colonial delegates in Charlotte, under the leadership of Colonel Thomas Polk, declared that Great Britain had: "wantonly trampled on our rights and liberties and inhumanly shed the innocent blood of American patriots at Lexington," and, that we "dissolve the political bands which have connected us to the mother country, " and, "we declare ourselves a free and independent people."

This Mecklenburg Declaration of Independence was affirmed by the militia leaders and was, therefore, binding upon Charlotteans. No doubt that this early act of insubordination and insurrection caught the ire of their British overseers. Thus, Charlotte's reputation as a hornet's nest was well deserved. The North Carolina DMV first started issuing First in Freedom license plates in 1975 upon the two hundred-year anniversary of the Mecklenburg Declaration of Independence.

At that time, North Carolina's First in Freedom plate was the only license plate offered until 1979. Other options were offered at that time after a Navy veteran, James Flowers of Hillsboro, NC, correctly asserted that "no southern state was first in freedom for black people."[11] Emancipation for blacks would not be made legal until the Emancipation Proclamation of President Abraham Lincoln was signed into law on January 1, 1863. Sadly, it would take two more years of civil war before the southern confederacy realized the necessity of submitting to Lincoln's ruling. It would be just over one hundred years later, after the Emancipation Proclamation of 1863, that Black people were granted the full legal rights and freedoms afforded to American citizens. But even with this slow progression of human rights, America has proven, over time, to be a land of equal opportunity for all as envisioned by out nation's founders and set forth in our founding documents; the Declaration of Independence and the US Constitution.

But beyond the bellicose sentiments of the Mecklenburg County Scots-Irish in those early years, there was also an independent religious streak which they developed as Presbyterians who had been oppressed by the State Church of England. Once removed to Ireland, the Presbyterian scots would once again be marginalized by the Catholic majority in Northern Ireland. These scrappy Scots-Irish, who made their way down the Appalachian chain from Pennsylvania, eagerly settled in the Charlotte-Mecklenburg region hoping for the freedom they had long sought.

The Reverend Billy Graham, arguably Charlotte's most famous son, descended from these same roots. He grew up in Calvary Presbyterian Church, where my grandparents raised my mother from her childhood. Patriotism, religious piety, hard work, and neighborliness were common virtues. Undoubtedly, these values rubbed off on me; if only by osmosis.

A deep connection with the land and a willingness to protect one's property characterized these early citizen farmers who often lived remotely from others and had to depend upon themselves for food and security. Consequently, there is a long tradition of gun ownership, hunting, and a sense of responsibility for the defense of one's family. When some folks criticize these who still cling to "guns and religion" as a recent American president was recorded saying, such things are actually inherent within the culture and traditions of much of the country and the Charlotte, North Carolina region is, historically, among such places.[12]

I remember, even as a small child, going squirrel hunting every Thanksgiving morning on the Garrison land in the Mallard Creek area of Mecklenburg County with cousins and uncles who had farmed the land after these many generations. We walked through the tall hardwood forests stopping every so often to be still and listen for squirrels stirring in the leafless treetops. I recall that the dairy farm and surrounding land was reduced in size over time until there was really no room to hunt any more. I must have been in my mid-teen years the last time we squirrel hunted on the old Garrison property. The University of North Carolina at Charlotte was buying the land and our hunting days on that property had come to an end. On the last hunt, I saw what I thought was a squirrel bed high up in a tree. I took a shot to clip the outer edge of the nest with our Winchester 22 caliber pump action rifle, in order to cause any squirrel inside the nest to move out into the open for a clear shot.

To my surprise, the squirrel nest stood up on its hind legs and hissed at me from above. It wasn't a squirrel nest, after all, but rather a large and angry racoon. It was apparent that I had at least nicked the raccoon, so I thought I should go ahead and put it out of its apparent misery. Sadly, racoons do not go down easily from 22 caliber rounds at that distance. I had to shoot the large racoon quite a few more times before it gave up the ghost and toppled from the tree. I remember feeling sad for what I had done.

I'm not sure if it was the pangs of transitioning through the mid-teen years into young adulthood, or knowing that we would not be able to hunt any longer on this rapidly developing tract of land, or the unnecessary death I had inflicted upon such a grand and unsuspecting creature. Perhaps it was all of these threads woven together that had evoked within me a deep sense of sorrow and an awareness that the wheels of time were turning. This sadness I felt was in stark contrast to the feeling of freedom and adventure that I usually experienced being outdoors in the woods.

From the time I was eight years old, I had lived, for several years, as an adventurer on par with the characters Daniel Boone and Davy Crockett, as played by Fess Parker in the movies and records I had loved as a young child. Even in kindergarten when we took turns bringing a favorite "record" to hear during nap time, my choice was always my Davy Crocket Album soundtrack and I knew those stories well. I don't think it was a big hit among the female demographic in our kindergarten class, but the boys liked it and in kindergarten that was all that mattered.[13]

You might say I was obsessed with the pioneer life. I had a coonskin cap, some fringed Indian style clothing, a collection of toy edged weapons, and an array of firearms ranging from pop guns, cap guns, and a BB gun that surprisingly never put my, or anyone else's, eye out. And did we have BB gun wars? I shudder now to think about it. But at least we had established rules of engagement for our collective safety. No shooting above the neck. That was the only rule. A groin shot was a bonus achievement! Oh, yes, and don't tell your parents; that was the only other rule in the rough and tumble frontier of Charlotte's Shannon Park neighborhood in those days. We would run wild through the diminishing woods that surrounded our Charlotte neighborhood. We particularly enjoyed playing, and staging battles, in and around the creek that ran through our neighborhood. Moral of the story: Never trust a seven-year old with a BB-gun; however earnest his pleas may seem.

For kids in our age range, that small fringe beyond civilization seemed something like the Amazon River that was occasionally featured on my favorite weekly television show, *The Wild Kingdom.* Every Friday night I was on the edge of my seat to await the adventures of popular zoologists Marlin Perkins and Jim Fowler. The show ran from 1963-88 and was sponsored by the Mutual of Omaha Insurance Company. We only had three TV channels in those days. There were no cell phones, no computers, and no video games. We had to create our fun and it seemed to come natural for me.

I was on a T-ball team, the Bees, in a Kid's league sponsored by the YMCA at the Johnson Y in Charlotte. Baseball was fun, and I was pretty good. But it was not as much fun as was exploring. I recall that on one lovely spring afternoon, when I had a T-Ball practice scheduled for later in the day, I asked my mom if I could go play in the creek with a friend. She complied with my request as the creek was very near to our home. My playmate and I caught a few crawdads and then I boldly made the brilliant suggestion that we set out to find the other end of the creek. We had played around the crawdad hole often but we had never gone much further downstream. For some unexplainable reason, at the wise age of seven, I felt the unquenchable urge to see where the creek led. Where did it end? Maybe there were bigger crawdads, or even snakes, further on up there? With little resistance from my partner in exploration, with whom I was supposed to carpool to T-Ball Practice within the hour, we began our adventure.

Exhilaration, curiosity, and youthful energy propelled us further up the creek than we ever intended to go, and we never found its mysterious terminus. At some point, we sensed the necessity to return and with a begrudging U-turn, we began the long trek home. Splashing back upstream through the creek, little did we suspect that our trek would lead us right into the jaws of discipline and possible death. All the while, I had little awareness of elapsed time and was incognizant of the serious trouble brewing back at home. Several hours after our initial departure, we arrived home at 1500 Shannonhouse Drive in Charlotte, having missed T-Ball practice by well over an hour. We did, however, make it home before dark, and I'm obviously still here to tell the story.

It is an important part of my background that I was raised in a churchgoing family, but I would not say that I was a Christian until the age of 16. My family was characterized by our Baptist orientation with regular church attendance, by a Christian moralism, and Southern manners, but, like the faith of many people, it was more about religion than a relationship with God. The Bible Belt, in those days, was characterized, in many ways, by this type of cultural Christianity. The Church, in general, was often more of a social institution than a spiritual hub. Church, for many, was more about your friends than your friendship with God.

My mother would later insightfully recall that our church was a bit more like a Christian country club than a Biblical model of what church is supposed to be. Though she loved her church, and her friends at church, she sensed in retrospect that something had been lacking, at least in our lives. She would comment, in retrospect, that in the 1970s through the early 80's, she didn't recall a strong emphasis upon the clear teaching of scripture nor a consistent emphasis upon Jesus's love for all people.

In 1982, we had a new pastor, Charles Page, come to First Baptist Charlotte and he brought in new staff, including a twenty-something youth pastor named Don Brock. In a Southern Baptist church, where each congregation is autonomous, the church forms its own pulpit search committee consisting of around a dozen members, usually active and prominent, who reviewed resumes, visited other churches incognito, and ultimately settled upon one candidate to steal from another sister congregation. The search committee's choice is typically for a candidate who resides far enough away to avoid any resentment from the sister congregation over losing their pastor. In this maneuvering, the Search Committee earnestly seeks the blessing of God. Seriously though, one would hope that God providentially works through the process to further His kingdom on earth.

My clear recollection is that something was noticeably different about the new pastor, our new youth pastor, and the interns that gave assistance to the youth ministry, which was characterized by exciting new activities and time spent hanging out with these dynamic young adult Christian leaders. At the age of 16 years old, I remember thinking that these people were possibly angels. I knew that they possessed something of a spiritual nature that I did not possess. Not too much later, as I developed better spiritual discernment and was invited to roll several homes of church members with toilet paper, I concluded that they were not at all actual angels. But yet there was something undeniably different about the new leadership regime that I had not noticed in others before. My mother commented that they were full of the Holy Spirit. My dad seemed pleased and had a renewed energy as he fulfilled his duties as a deacon in the church. But for me, and little did I know it, nor had I given any thought to it, I was still lost spiritually and I had not made the transition from a natural man to a spiritual man, as the Bible distinguishes.[14] In short, I had not yet crossed the line of faith.

As I would later learn upon the *Saratoga*, there is a clear line of demarcation in the life of a U.S. Navy sailor when his or her ship crosses the equator. Dating at least four centuries back in the western seafaring tradition, sailors are initiated with all sorts of hazing rites that are apparently fun for the ones doing the initiating. When I crossed the equator on the *Saratoga* on the 10th of December, 1985, those who had never crossed (known as Pollywogs) made up the majority of the crew. Those who had previously crossed the line and had been initiated (known as Shellbacks) superintended over us Pollywogs in the Line Crossing ceremony. We were subjected to various "character building activities" like swimming underwater in large (maybe twenty yards long) and three feet deep metal containers filled with a nuclear-looking green liquid of unknown composition. The object was to stay under the water as you swam from one end of the container to the other so that you would not get whacked on the head with a fire hose. It helped to completely ignore the floating garbage and other unidentifiable objects that had been cast into the green liquid.

Another exercise involved crawling through a long tunnel of heavy nylon fabric. Somehow the rotten garbage and food refuse from the mess decks had been shoveled into the long tarp like tunnel that was barely big enough for a fat man to crawl through. As before, just keep your head down and move forward. This, too, shall pass. There were a few other rites of passage in the Shellback initiation that I shall leave unmentioned. Suffice it to say, however, that when it was all said and done, and it took nearly a full-day mind you, all of us pollywogs were greatly relieved. The grand finale was to rip off your disgusting work uniform and stand under fire hoses pointed down from forklifts on the flight deck so as to wash off any unhealthy remnants of biohazardous material. In retrospect, it was a great time and another highlight of the cruise.

But in a spiritually analogous way, the transition from Pollywog to Shellback is something akin to the spiritual transformation that Jesus talked about when He said: "You must be born again. You cannot see the Kingdom of God unless you are born again."[15] In fact, the entire New Testament of the *Holy Bible* affirms the idea and necessity of each person experiencing a new beginning in the faith for themselves. The Apostle Paul summed it up well, when he cited the universal sin nature affecting every human being and followed that sobering appraisal by saying: "But because of His great love for us, God, who is rich in mercy made us alive in Christ even when we were dead in transgressions – it is by grace that you have been saved." (Ephesians 2:4-5) After that, in verses 8-9, the apostle explained to neophyte Christians: "For by grace you have been saved through faith, and that not of yourselves; it is the gift of God so that no one can boast."

Up until August of 1982, there is no doubt that I was a spiritual pollywog. My first baptism at the age of seven had been no more advantageous to me than going for a swim. Church was just a place to go because my family went. I had relationships with church folk but did not yet have a personal relationship with God. By the time the First Baptist Church of Charlotte, North Carolina had called its new pastor and youth pastor in 1982, I was a sophomore at Independence High School. The poor choices I was making by that time in my life were mounting and I was, spiritually speaking, lost at sea. I would soon undergo an authentic spiritual transformation in the summer of 1982, that would be even much more delineating and defining than my Shellback initiation. Little did I know, when my home church began this exciting new era under the leadership of Charles Page and Don Brock, I would soon experience the spiritual rebirth that Jesus Christ talked about, and that experience, itself, would change everything.

CHAPTER 6

AN ANCHOR IN THE SOUL

By the summer after my sophomore year of high school, our youth group at church was planning its annual end of summer youth retreat in the Blue Ridge mountains at Camp Cheerio in Glade Valley, North Carolina. It was an opportunity to get away from home for a week and do a range of things that teenagers often do. Based upon past precedent, there were also possibilities of romancing, cigar smoking, and sneaking out of cabins at night for those not faint of heart. I had developed a long running friendship with a classmate, Brian Freeze, since the seventh grade. By the tenth grade we had already experienced many adventures and, surprisingly, were still alive to tell about them. Clearly though, in more than a few cases, it was in our best interest to maintain strict confidentiality. Early on, we had perfected a well-oiled scam in which I told my mother that I was going to spend the night with Brian, and he reciprocated by telling his mother that he was going to spend the night with me.

I am not sure why I chose a rebellious path. The Prophet Isaiah offered telling insight when he declared: "We all, like sheep, have gone astray, each one of us has turned to our own way...." As

I recall the first time Brian and I pulled the spend-the-night stunt, we were around thirteen and it was the summer after our seventh-grade year. Resourcefully, we had arranged transportation over to Brian's former neighborhood, Fairfield Plantation, where we would bivouac overnight at the neighborhood tennis & swim club. Why we felt compelled to throw all of the lounge chairs into the pool, I cannot say with certainty. On these occasional overnight excursions, we rarely slept. I vividly remember nearly freezing to death at least twice. I guess it was the sense of freedom, adventure, and thrill that came from being on our own with no supervision that was most appealing.

Really, on the first of such occasions, one would think that we would have learned our lesson and chosen a different path going forward. But at the young age of thirteen, and just beyond, such lessons are not easily learned. The all-nighter in Fairfield Plantation resulted in total disaster.

It must have been sometime after midnight, when we had a run in with some bad actors who were far worse than us. I can tell you from memory that sleep does not come easily upon pool cabana picnic tables after numerous caffeinated drinks and candy bars from a vending machine. So, we decided to roam around the neighborhood to see what interesting things we might discover. To our surprise; we were not the only predators out late on that summer night.

Brian and I came upon a carload of older dudes who had quietly pulled up beside a parked car on the curb alongside a home with a nicely manicured lawn where, presumably, everyone was asleep. We watched from the shadows as these young men inserted what appeared to be a section of a garden hose into the gas tank of the parked car and then gave a suck to the other end. That was certainly puzzling...so we decided to move in for a closer look. Apparently, Brian and I had a startling effect upon those guys, and they were not too happy about our sudden and unannounced presence. They quickly assessed our age range and, with some language that was not flattering, we were told that we were to be detained until such time as they finished siphoning the gas from the resident's car. You are doing "what," we asked? "We are stealing gas," they replied. Then, it dawned on us that we were part of a crime scene and were at the mercy of CRIMINALS! I can't tell you how exciting that was.

Really, looking back on my teen years, I am fortunate to be alive. Some of the decisions that we made, and I say we because rarely was I alone in my stupidity, could have resulted in our demise. I had loving parents, though perhaps a bit disengaged as they were both working full time jobs with dad commuting twenty miles one way downtown to Charlotte's First Union National Bank, while mom was a second-grade teacher at Clear Creek Elementary School. As I stated, we were impeccable in our church attendance. My parents were about as straitlaced as they came, and no one could accuse them of being overly strict or, knowingly, over permissive. I had no doubts as to their love and support of me, and still I acted out in ways that now cause me to cringe in disbelief.

But, unfortunately, I have no recollection of any clear sense of genuine Christian presence, beyond the "Churchianity," with which I was inundated. During my ninth-grade year at Northeast Jr. High School, I was on the school's varsity football team and we achieved the title of Eastern League Champions in the Charlotte Mecklenburg School System with a seven-win and zero-loss record. It was an extraordinary year and there is no doubt that we had good coaching. The head coach, whom I will leave unnamed, would gather the team before every game for a recitation of the Lord's Prayer from Matthew chapter 7. No sooner had we said

"Amen," that the head coach would cuss a blue streak the likes of which I don't think I ever heard in the Navy. Coach would get in our faces and cuss at us with Red Man chewing tobacco juice punctuating the profanity, which must have proven motivational given the success of our season. It was this very type of cultural Christianity in which I was enveloped that cause me to disregard it as anything truly worthwhile or meaningful.

Then came the new pastor and staff to our church and things seemed to be different with them. By the time of the summer youth retreat after my sophomore year of high school, my poor choices had taken me even farther from the Christian path. As the week at camp progressed, along with the usual shenanigans, the youth pastor asked us to make a "sin-list," while explaining that all have sinned and come short of the glory of God. We were promised anonymity and confidentiality with regard to this sin-list; it was to be between us and God. We were supposed to be introspective and seek the leadership of God in our spiritual inventory. I don't remember taking it, the 'sin-list' thing, too seriously. But I do remember the moments when we were given time to ourselves, to get away from others, in order to reflect upon prescribed Bible verses and to consider our relationship with God. Even as one who was spiritually blind at the time, the views of the Blue Ridge mountains from Camp Cheerio had a way of speaking to the heart about transcendent matters.

The next to last night at camp, probably Wednesday night, our youth group of around a hundred students, from 7th-12th grade plus some college kids who were along as interns, were gathered in a large room with a large wooden cross as the focal point. Our youth pastor spoke about confessing and repenting of our sins. We were reminded of the 'sin-list' that we had been instructed to keep that week in our scheduled personal devotional time. I simply recall that many of the students, who were my peers, appeared to be emotionally affected by the message and the call to change our ungodly ways in repentance. We were invited to come to the front of the room, if we wished, to nail our 'sin-list' to the cross in accordance with what Jesus, God's Son, had done for us in bearing our sins upon a similar cross. The mood and tempo moved steadily to the shedding of tears and people hugging one another, particularly the girls. But as the evening wore on it seemed that almost everyone had taken an intentional walk to the cross except me and a few others.

Sadly, I recall being skeptical. I had seen similar displays of emotion on the last night of previous youth retreats. Such things were rather obligatory...or at least expected in a Baptist youth retreat in those days. Honestly, my recollection is that I felt nothing that night and I had given the matter of my sin very little thought over the course of the week. I do remember thinking to myself that if I was a real Christian, I would probably not be smoking pot and drinking alcohol with my party-friends, as I was in the habit of doing at that time in my life. But that realization and admission, in itself, was more thought than I had ever given the matter before that week in August 1982 at Camp Cheerio. In retrospect, this was actual progress, even if not much. So, perhaps as one of the last holdouts, I made my way to the front of the room and nailed my 'sin-list' to the cross.

But nothing happened and I must have thought that once I went through the act of nailing the sin-list to the cross, I would feel what everyone else appeared to be feeling. Yet I had no tears. There was no great impulse to hug anyone beyond my casual interest in a few of the girls that was surely unrelated to the exercise at hand. My lack of experience, as anticipated from my observation of others, concerned me. So afterward, I went to talk with Don Brock, the youth pastor. Though new to his position in our church, Don seemed approachable and, after all, he had established this whole "nail your sin-list to the cross" scenario.

Truly, my lack of feeling anything tangible or different, in contrast to the apparent experience of some of my peers, was increasingly a cause of concern to me. In response to my stated concern, Don said something like: "I think this will all make more sense tomorrow. Tonight, you confessed your sins. Tomorrow night you will have the opportunity to fill that void with something better." That is what I recall, but it is likely that he also gave me a foreshadowing of the gospel, which is that "God was in Christ reconciling the world to Himself and not counting our sins against us." The next day would be the day that I would finally grasp the reality of God's love for me and respond to His love with repentance and faith.

The final full day at Camp Cheerio was Friday, and we had more time to enjoy the beauty of the mountain top experience of clear blue skies with a visibility of nearly fifty miles. The temperature was pleasant at three thousand feet above sea-level and the horses kept by the YMCA Camp only added to the sense of being somewhere clean, pristine, and almost magical. That afternoon, I recall a Bible study led by the senior pastor, who had just driven up to Camp Cheerio from Charlotte with his wife, Sandra Page.

Dr. Charles Page had recently come to First Baptist Charlotte from the First Baptist Church of North Augusta, South Carolina. Not long after his arrival, Dr. Page invited Don Brock to join the staff as the Youth Minister at FBC Charlotte. With these two, things seemed to be beyond business as usual for the congregation of Charlotte's First Baptist Church, and for the youth ministry program as well. Dr. Page's teaching from the Bible that Friday afternoon from the second chapter of the book of First Corinthians brought me to a clearer realization that I was not a Christian in the Biblical sense. That passage of Scripture includes these words from 1 Corinthians 2:14: "The person without the Holy Spirit does not accept the things that come from the Spirit of God but considers them foolishness and cannot understand them because they are discerned only through the Spirit." Through the pastor's teaching on the carnal nature of people just like me and the necessity of a spiritual intervention by the Holy Spirit; I began to rightly classify myself as a lost person in need of Jesus Christ.

On the last day of camp, our youth minister explained our individual need for Jesus as our personal Lord and Savior. It was clearly communicated that this was a personal choice that we must make individually. This was not just about a display of emotion or going along with the crowd. In fact, Don asked those who wanted to receive Christ to come down individually and kneel before God in a prayer of commitment and a public profession of faith. I have no idea if I was first, last, or the only one who went down to that altar that morning. I do recall that the sun streaked in from the windows illuminating the beautiful wood-sided high-ceilinged meeting hall. I also recall feeling almost swept up and taken down to the altar, as if something greater than myself was present and active. I knelt and prayed, in my own words, inviting Christ to be the Lord of my life.

After supper, and as daylight gave way to darkness, Don directed the boys to stand together on one small hill while the girls, with their chaperones, stood on a similar rise with a slight valley separating us by about sixty yards. The girls, led by Don's wife Mary, sang hymns and choruses that we had learned during the week and the boys sang, as led by our student ministry Intern Jeff Warren, to echo the girls. Some songs we sang together in unison. I had never experienced the sudden awareness that God was actually real, as I clearly felt during the singing of those praise songs that evening.

The next day, I would leave Camp Cheerio to return home to Charlotte as a different person. The Scripture describes true believers in this way: "If anyone is in Christ, he is a new creation; old things are passed away and all things have become new." (2 Corinthians 5:17)

When I returned from camp, I recall an emerging awareness of several things: first, that God was real, secondly, that I was a different person now, and, thirdly, that I needed to change some things about my life. When I explained this to my best friend, Brian, who had also been on the youth trip and had likewise made a public profession of faith, he seemed somewhat surprised by my new resolutions. While we had been hell-raisers together since the seventh grade, I was now focused upon heaven. That he did not seem to have the lasting resolve that I had brought home from camp was a concern, as well as a mystery to me. Chris, another friend from my high school who had come with us to camp, did not seem to be impacted by the experience, as I had been. To his credit, Chris, a dedicated athlete, was not nearly as oriented to the wild life as Brian and I had been. But still, his apathy about my new spiritual orientation was perplexing to me.

I recall going into the Record Bar, a music store that sold albums, audio cassettes, and yes...8 track tapes, on the corner of Independence Boulevard and Albemarle Road. A black friend of mine from Independence High School was working at Record Bar that day. As it was the end of the summer vacation and we had not seen each other for over two months, there was the usual banter of catching up on summer happenings. I shared with Nathan how I had received Christ as my savior and was at the Record Bar to find some Christian music instead of my normal diet of rock music. At that time, the early '80s, there were only a very few artists producing contemporary music with a Christian message. And I had been unfamiliar with those few Christian musicians until my week at Camp Cheerio. Suffice it to say that Nathan had never heard of Amy Grant and, knowing me as he did, he also seemed puzzled by my confession of faith.

It was obvious that I really had my work cut out for me at Independence High School with the apparent spiritual unawareness before me. And it would be another year, 1983, before the heavy metal Christian group Stryper, a Christian version of the rock band KISS, would wow crowds with inspirational and thought-provoking songs such as: "To Hell with the Devil." Seriously though, compared with more recent times, there just were not many Christian resources available to believers back in those days. Specifically, there were not many Christian resources geared towards youth that seemed to connect with a younger culture. Too many churches seemed locked into forms and styles that were common to the 1950-70s, if not earlier.

Another challenge to my spiritual development was the fact that I lived and went to school in a different part of the county than most of my church friends at First Baptist Charlotte. At that time, and to my knowledge, there were not any dynamic churches in the southeast part of the Charlotte area which fed into Independence High School. Independence Sr High was, then, the largest High School in North Carolina with some 2,500 students in grades 10-12. Our caricatured reputation at the Big "I" in those days was that we drove tractors to school. In truth, the area was a bit more rural than the areas around East Mecklenburg, South Meck, and Myers Park High Schools where most of my church friends from First Baptist Charlotte went to school. But the tractor rumor was way off the mark. I never saw anyone drive a tractor to school. Everyone there knew that tractors were for odd-jobs during after school hours.

The kids at my high school included newly relocated suburbanites like my family, who had moved into the large Farmwood Subdivision that stretched along the borders of an 18-hole golf course known as Pine Lake Country Club. There were a good number of other subdivisions in the area as well. Most of these kids had moved with their families into the area in the 1970s and '80s from nearby Charlotte and other more distant places like upstate New York. A good few of our classmates had moved down south as a result of a large IBM workforce relocation. Then there were the local kids in the town of Mint Hill and its environs. Some of these families had lived and worked in the area for generations. Some of the long-term residents were black, but most of these were kids from working class white families.

Almost all of the minority population kids were bused in from the nine-miles distant Barrington Oaks apartment complex off the Plaza or further away in parts of West Charlotte. In 1973, Charlotte had embarked on a busing strategy in an effort to integrate schools which led to some kids in white neighborhoods being bused to schools in black neighborhoods, while some kids in black neighborhoods were being bused to schools in white neighborhoods. As I recall, and I started public school in the Charlotte Mecklenburg School System in 1972-73, black and white kids generally got along well together regardless of race. Even if most of us went home to different parts of town, after the school day was over, we were just fellow-students that fate had brought together. Most of our waking hours were spent together. Some of my close friends over the twelve years of public school were black.

But churches were largely a different story then with regard to integration. The late Dr. Martin Luther King, Jr. observed: "It is appalling that the most segregated hour of Christian America is eleven o'clock on Sunday morning." While we had some black people from the continent of Africa in the congregation of First Baptist Charlotte, there were few, if any, American-born blacks in our congregation in those days. Interestingly, we had a highly esteemed elderly black church custodian named Cleve Davenport, who lived in an apartment on the expansive church campus even though his working days were clearly behind him. I never remember hearing any racial demagoguery from my family, church friends, or even my school friends.

My mother, an elementary school teacher with a gift to teach reading, would volunteer time at the Boy's Club adjacent to the Barrington Oaks Apartments, which fed into Clear Creek Elementary School, where she taught second grade. To recall my busy working mom driving over to the Boy's Club at the Barrington Oaks Apartments to volunteer as a tutor to her young black school children after hours is remarkable to me. I also remember my dad saying once, with great emotion, that sometimes the black women were treated poorly at First Union National Bank, where he often worked alongside them in clerical duties. That must have been in the early 1980s. My parents always welcomed black friends, and people of other races and cultures, and they were accepting and kind to all people.

It is still a wonder to me that I had drifted so far from the positive moral example of my parents to the indifferent hell-raiser that I had become by the age of 16, and before my Christian conversion in the summer of '82. Dad had been a deacon in the church and an impeccably faithful church attender while my mom had taught Sunday School and previously sang in the choir. Yet the substance of their Christian faith had been more from habit in the type of cultural Christianity so common in the Bible belt in those days. When I came back from Camp Cheerio as "a new creation in Christ," all things were indeed new. I began to read my Bible with great interest and insight, whereas before the good book had no attraction to me whatsoever.

The most memorable, and mysterious, occurrence looking back upon it all, was the experience I had shortly after returning from Camp Cheerio. I don't recall the exact catalyst, but I am fairly certain it involved prayer and the reading of Scripture; which were increasingly characteristic of my new life in Christ at that time. I can only remember being in the living room of our home, with no one else present at the time, and being overcome by a strong sense of conviction of my sins prior to my recent conversion at Camp Cheerio. It seemed that the full weight of my sin and rebellion against God was revealed to me, and I could only weep with great remorse and regret. The righteousness, love, and presence of God was completely overwhelming to me and it seemed that something significant was taking place in my spiritual life, which was increasingly the center of my existence.

The Baptist Faith and Message, Southern Baptist's Confession of Faith since 1925, though revised and updated twice since that time, says of repentance: "Repentance is a genuine turning from sin toward God. Faith is the acceptance of Jesus Christ and commitment of the entire personality to Him as Lord and Savior." Theologians have long contemplated the mystery of the Ordo Salutis, which is Latin for "order of salvation." While much more has been written than is warranted on this occasion, suffice it to say that the elements of God's initiative, the hearing of the gospel of Jesus Christ, the convicting work of the Holy Spirit, and a response of repentance and faith are generally agreed upon as essential to authentic Christian conversion. In John's gospel chapter three, Jesus likened the new birth to the wind, "which blows where it pleases. You hear its sound, but you cannot tell where it comes from or where it is going. So is everyone who is born of the Spirit." Nicodemus, a religious leader, was confused by Jesus' words and asked how he, as an old man, could be born again? Nicodemus' response of uncertainty and outright confusion reveals the otherworldly nature of Christian conversion. Paul the apostle would even refer to salvation as a mystery that has now been revealed.

Reflecting the predominant Reformed theological stream in the Southern Baptist heritage, the *Baptist Faith and Message*, as recorded in 1925 and retained through the most recent version in 2000, says: "Election is the gracious purpose of God, according to which He regenerates, justifies, sanctifies, and glorifies sinners. It is the glorious display of God's sovereign goodness, which is infinitely wise, holy, and unchangeable. It excludes boasting and promotes humility." Of my own salvation experience, I can only say that, God worked within me to bring me to an understanding of my lost condition and my need for the grace and forgiveness that God offers through His Son Jesus Christ. Though I am not certain of the exact spiritual mechanics of my conversion experience, there is no doubt that it was as if an anchor was lifted from my soul. The lostness and spiritual blindness that had long kept me from God had been removed and replaced with newfound grace. John Newton, the writer of the long-popular hymn, *Amazing Grace*, declared: "I once was lost, but now am found, was blind but now I see." The hymn goes on to say: Through many dangers, toils, and snares I have already come; 'Tis grace hath brought me safe thus far, and grace will lead me home." The lyrics of the well-known hymn summarized my experience with Christ and would mark my progression in the faith going forward. Though, some of the steps I would take moving forward would be a departure from the path so suddenly and unexpectedly set before me.

CHAPTER 7

DARKENED SHIP & DECEPTIVE RIGGING

One of the distinct characteristics of my term of service in the U.S. Navy was the Cold War rivalry between the United States and the Soviet Union. I suppose that for a young male at the seasoned age of eighteen, the ever-present reality of a thermonuclear war just didn't have the ominous tone one would rightly expect it to carry. Yet, I can tell you that in my experience, the Soviet rivalry was continually brought to our attention back in the days of my Active Duty service, from 1984-87. And I can also say, that at the age of 18, I never lost a wink of sleep over it. It is common knowledge that invincibility, and a lack of sensibility, are the chief characteristics of males at that age and this is why the armed services have been historically populated by this demographic group. Perhaps we, as young recruits, only considered that the Soviet rivalry was brought to our attention in order to give a sense of importance to all that we were doing in our military training.

At Great Lakes Recruit Training Command, where I reported on 14 July 1984, the Cold War contest was immediately set before us in the starkest of terms. I remember our Company Commander directing our Company 219 in marching cadence songs as we marched every-where we went from Reveille at 0500 to Taps at 2200. We marched quite often and at times it seemed certain that we marched just to march. One thing that made marching less monotonous was the cadence songs to which we marched. Some of the marching songs even referred to our military rivalry with the Soviets and no one could lead us in marching as well as our Lead Company Commander Chief Bussell.

Chief Bussell had a second in command whose rate (job), rank, and name was Mess Specialist Petty Officer First Class Gallero (MS1 Gallero). Like Chief Bussell, and all of the Company Commanders, Petty Officer Gallero was always "squared away." Petty Officer Gallero's English was characterized with the thick Filipino accent of his home nation, the Philippines, which was formerly a U.S. Territory. In fact, there were a good number of Filipinos in the Navy in those days and there was a very large U.S. Naval Base at Subic Bay in the Philippines, that also served as a recruiting station. I had a number of Filipino friends during my enlistment, including my time on the *Saratoga*. Like our #2 Company Commander, MS1 Gallero, Filipinos often served as Mess Specialists in the Navy, which put them way up the social collateral food chain (pun intended). Bluntly put, the Mess Specialists were among the most highly valuable social assets on a Naval warship due to the authority they commanded over everything from cinnamon buns to the occasional steak and lobster dinner, which we were served on rare occasions.

One of the distinct linguistic idiosyncrasies of the Filipino brogue spoken by Petty Officer Gallero was that he pronounced his "f's" as "p's." Unfortunately, his favorite, and most often used swear word was the "f" word which always came out, unintentionally, as a "p" word. That he always added a string of other off-color anatomical terms after his slightly skewed use of the "f" word made it all the more comical. But whatever you did, you would dare not laugh but once, and suffice it to say that Chief Bussell did not delegate the calling of marching cadence to Petty Officer Gallero a second time. That distinct honor fell to the Chief himself, and he did it quite well. Chief Bussell, a black man with a clear rich voice and energetic rhythm, led us in singing cadences that made marching almost fun. But of course, we were careful not to let him think we were anywhere close to having fun, so that we would not be punished for the thought.

It went something like this: Chief Bussell would sing (I don't know what else to call it) and then we would repeat or reply with a response which he had taught us. These songs included favorites like: "We're not the Army, the back-packing Army!" "We're not the Marines; they only look mean!" "We're not the Coast Guard; they don't even work hard!" "We're not the Air Force, the slow-flying Air Force!" "We are the NAVY, The World's Finest Navy!" "Am I right or wrong? You're Right!!!!" "Are we Weak or Strong? We're Strong!!!" "One, Two, Three, Four: One, Two, Three, Four!" on "One," your left foot better be hitting the ground, on "Two," (right foot) on "Three" (left foot) then "Four (right foot) ... maybe you get the idea? For months after boot camp, I would occasionally wake up in a cold sweat with my legs marching to that cadence.

But it was always a crowd-pleaser to sing along with Chief Bussell asserting our superiority above the other branches of service while boasting of our greatness, and the young men of Company 219 perfected the art. I almost hesitate to mention it, but another little ditty that Chief Bussell worked into our marching song playlist included the phrase: "Kill a Commie for Uncle Ronnie!" Of course, with the classroom instruction we were receiving on things ranging from Naval history to the present chain of command, we knew that Uncle Ronnie was no less than our present Commander in Chief. By the summer of 1984 Ronald Reagan, the 40th President of the United States, was hitting his stride and the Soviets were intent upon matching him step for step in order to outpace the U.S. in the Arms race as well as to achieve global supremacy of Communism over Democracy. So it was, from the beginning of our training, that we were being programmed to engage the Soviets in the Cold War contest that would be at its apex by the time we would hit the fleet.

In OS "A" School, I clearly remember our primary instructor accentuating the importance of what we were being trained to do in Combat Information Center by telling us that a Soviet submarine with nuclear weapons was on station just off of the United States coastline. He went on to explain that the boundary line of International Waters was twelve miles from a nation's coastline. The Instructor told us that a Soviet sub with nuclear missiles was always on patrol just outside of that 12-mile line in International waters and that the sub cruised continually just off our coastline from New York to Cape Canaveral Florida and back again. When that sub was done with its six-month deployment, another would replace it and the threat level would be sustained.

Later, after I reported to the USS *Saratoga*, we were often reminded of the U.S. Soviet rivalry as we engaged in drills to prepare us for possible conflict and battle. A sea-going U.S. naval warship works though cycles that center around preparation, deployment, return, and refit, then it begins the preparation for deployment again. The U.S.-Soviet contest was a constant factor as we were doing battle training for our approaching Mediterranean deployment. All recruits were taught in boot camp to use a gas mask and, there, we were subjected to a real gas chamber. Back in boot camp we were lined up to proceed through the gas chamber after being instructed to put the mask on and take it off under duress. This real type simulation allowed us to experience first-hand the effects of tear gas, which is commonly used in the boot camps of the various branches of the military in order to simulate nuclear biological chemical attacks in preparation for worst-case battle scenarios.

In pre-deployment, U.S. Navy warships go through an intense training phase, which we referred to as workups, and these were held in an operating area off of the coast of Guantanamo Bay, Cuba. The U.S. Naval Base at Guantanamo Bay (AKA GITMO) is home base to a host of ship, submarine, air-squadron, and shore-duty personnel whose job it is to simulate war with U.S. Navy ships and air-squadrons preparing for active deployment. The base itself is a secluded enclave protected by hills that surround the Bay and make it a citadel on the south end of the island of Cuba.

The U.S. claimed rights to this valuable property since seizing it in 1898 during the Spanish-American War. In 1903, the U.S. and Cuba signed a lease allowing the U.S. to use the land upon which the Naval Base and Internment Camp for Terrorists stands to this day. Needless to say, the Communist Government of Cuba, which overtook the Island of Cuba in the Communist Revolution of 1959, does not recognize the 1903 Agreement and the U.S. presence is a sore spot for the present Cuban regime. Reportedly, even in their national poverty, the Cuban Government does not cash the rent checks that the U.S. still doles out to them in keeping with the 1903 Agreement.

In the forty plus years of it's active service; the USS *Saratoga*, and it's Crew, would earn two of the highly coveted Battle "E" Ribbons (for Excellence) for its meticulously graded performance during work-ups at Guantanamo Bay Cuba, and one of those would be in 1985 as our Ship prepared for its upcoming deployment. It was during these interactive drills and simulated experiences known collectively as "War Games" at GITMO, that the conflict with the Soviet Union was again strongly impressed upon us, particularly those of us who worked in the Combat Information Center. The combat aircraft of Navy squadrons stationed at GITMO that we engaged in War Games were simulating Soviet MIG's, while U.S. subs and ships out of GITMO were playing the part of Soviet vessels of war against us in planned and simulated adversarial exercises.

I don't recall many of the details of the tedious blur that is known far and wide to sailors as GITMO War Games but suffice it to say that we only got two or three hours of sleep a day at best during those several days of exercises. And quite noticeably, our typical at-sea routines were dramatically amped up with long hours at General Quarters Battle Stations, nearly round the clock Flight Operations, and a general sense that we had better not screw anything up. But in the end, the *Saratoga* must have collectively excelled to the extent that we were awarded the coveted Battle "E" Ribbon. Just as importantly, we were also given the signature "Mighty Fine" appraisal from Captain Unruh over the ship's 1MC system. Both of these achievements made all of the stress and lack of sleep associated with War Games at GITMO worth our efforts.

Once we had completed the ten-day transit across "the Big Grey Pond," as the Atlantic Ocean was known to us, undoubtedly Soviet radar platformed upon ships and airplanes was tracking the USS *Saratoga*, and Soviet submarines were an ever-present concern. I'll never forget the exhilaration I felt when we passed through the Strait of Gibraltar, the sole point of entry from the West into the Mediterranean Sea. As it was the dark of night when the *Saratoga* transited into the Med, I was unable to see the Rock of Gibraltar, which stood 1,398 feet above sea level just off the *Saratoga*'s port side. Morocco, and the vast African continent was just off of our starboard side. The *Saratoga* charted a course near the center of the nine-mile strait and I managed to slip away from Combat Information Center to see with my own eyes what the radar scope and nautical charts revealed to us. Through the darkness my eyes beheld the mysterious contoured coastline on our port side in contrast to the near-distant coastline to starboard; which appeared nearly flat by comparison. Both beckoning shorelines were punctuated with similar shimmering lights, which always caused me, and sailors plying these waters over the centuries, to wonder about the inhabitants of these foreign lands.

To a nineteen-year old kid, who had rarely traveled beyond his home environs ranging from Myrtle Beach, South Carolina to Boone, North Carolina, this was a big deal! Just being out to sea; beyond the familiar sight of land was a big deal. With each nautical mile the *Saratoga* steamed eastward in the Med; unfamiliar coastline, ancient islands, and foreign nations awaited our progress. While the tranquil blue waters of the Caribbean Sea projected a sense of piratical history and cruise-boat luxury, the Med seemed to breath antiquity and it had a time machine-like quality to it that is unmatched anywhere else.

Various empires and kingdoms, including the Egyptians, the Israelites, the Assyrians, the Babylonians, the Persians, the Greeks, the Carthaginians, the Romans, on through the various European explorers in the Age of Discovery had all sailed these waters or marched armies along its coastline. More recently the Americans and the Soviets, along with lesser but armed proxy nations, were playing cat and mouse games that could easily escalate into pitched battle the likes of which could never have been imagined by our military predecessors.

And yet, some of the provocations between the U.S. and Soviet Navies actually had an almost comical nature to them. I remember a number of times a "fishing boat" got within close range of us in the Med and we knew it to be a confirmed Soviet craft for purposes of espionage. While the watercraft may have been made to look like a fishing boat, it was fitted with sophisticated listening devices. I'm not sure if it was our prowess in maintaining radio secrecy or the use of our jamming signals, but the Soviet "fishing boat" had to resort to merely going through our trash on several occasions. It was a known fact that ships were permitted to dispose of trash overboard beyond the fifty-mile mark from coastline. You can imagine how much trash was dumped from an aircraft carrier with 5,000 men.

You can be assured that we never threw anything of any intelligence value overboard, as security protocols prevented such actions. What in the world were the Soviet "fishermen" doing then, noticeably gathering and going through our trash? The word was that Playboy magazines were randomly placed in the bags just to get the Soviets to waste their time. Perhaps it was intended as an act of diplomacy. I've heard stories of U.S. and Soviet ships passing closely enough in open seas that the crews could moon one another. Thankfully, I do not recall anything like that ever happening on the *Saratoga* and it if it happened anywhere, it was likely upon smaller ships with less scrutiny and greater maneuverability than an aircraft carrier of our size.

One of the antics we did execute from time to time at night was the order to "Darken ship and rig deceptive lighting." Undoubtedly, this effort would have been of little value on a carrier against active radar which paints a blimp proportionate to the size of the vessel being tracked. But there must have been enough strategic value in steaming along less than friendly coastlines, or in the open sea, where we would benefit from being misperceived as a sailboat rather than the mega-warship that we in fact were. In "Darken ship and rig receptive lighting" conditions, all of the exterior lights on the *Saratoga* were extinguished and it was someone's job to rig up just enough lights to make the *Saratoga* appear as a sailboat.

Such deceptive countermeasures have long been part of military conflict and were recorded as far back as the 8th century B.C., when Homer recounts in the *Iliad* his tale of the Greek General Agamemnon who had the Trojan Horse rolled to the gates of Troy. The Greek soldiers delivered the large wooden horse to the Trojans, presumably as a parting gift to a long-time adversary, before saluting and turning westward towards home. The Trojans waited until they thought the coast was clear before rolling the gifted horse triumphantly into the city center. Congratulating themselves, they celebrated and went to bed late and inebriated. Little did they know that the wooden horse contained several courageous Greek soldiers who were to exit the façade after the city was in slumber, only to open the gates of Troy to the Greek invaders bivouacked out of sight but nearby.

In the Art of War, Sun Tzu, the 5th century Chinese general, military philosopher, and strategist said: "All of warfare is based upon deception. When we are able to attack, we must seem unable. When using our forces, we must appear inactive. When we are near, we must make the enemy believe we are far away. When far away, we must make him believe we are near." Thus, it was that our job in Combat Information Center was to be vigilant and, on the look-out for any signs of the presence or absence of our chief adversaries, the Soviets or their regional proxies. Our routines at sea were punctuated by regular Security Alert drills, which were to prepare our military response to the possibility of a Security Alert. When Tango Alpha was called, the sentries of our Marine detachment (around fifty Marines), were in absolute authority over our shipboard security.

Like General Quarters (GQ) battle stations; when Security Alert was called over the 1MC every sailor had instructions. For most, it was simply to stand fast and out of the way without any movement. The difference between GQ and Security Alert was that GQ was announced: "All Hands man your battle stations. Proceed forward and up on the starboard side, down and aft on the port Side." While General Quarters called the entire crew to Battle Stations, Security Alert was in response to the small-scale conflict of an unauthorized boarding of our ship with ill intent. Therefore, Security Alert was announced with as great of a sense of urgency as was GQ. The crew, at large, was directed to stand fast. The announcement reminded everyone that the Marine sentries had absolute control of the Ship. At that point, even the ship's Captain was under the authority of the Marine chain of command onboard the ship. The reality of it all was that Security Alert was to be called in response to a terrorist cell boarding the ship with the likely desire to obtain control over our most lethal form of weaponry.

Everyone onboard knew that we were carrying some serious arsenal in the event of a conflict with the Soviets. Though not with great frequency, while eating on the mess decks or walking through the Hangar Bay and other places, at any given time of the day or night you might come upon heavily armed Marine sentries with gas masks donned and bayonets affixed to their M-16 rifles. They would be in full camo battle dress to simulate a nuclear, biological, or chemical occurrence as they had their skin covered from head to toe. Anyone with any power of observation could see that these Marine Sentries were guarding long, pointed munitions. When asked if the *Saratoga* was carrying nuclear missiles, the response was always: "We can neither confirm nor deny the presence of nuclear weaponry onboard the USS *Saratoga*."

I will say it was an entertaining experience to watch the Marine response to a Security Alert Drill if you happened to be on the mess decks when the drill was called. Like most military drills, a Security Alert was usually called at the worst opportune time which was usually during traditional sleeping hours. If you happened to be going to the mess decks for mid-rats (midnight rations) and Security Alert was called, you were in the perfect place to see the Marines come storming up from beneath decks where their berthing compartment, arms, and equipment were located. Thankfully, in the event of a Security Alert Drill, they were required to at least wear their skivvies but that was apparently all that was operationally required. It was hysterical to see these guys come charging up the ladder and out of their berthing compartment armed to the teeth with Riot Style 12-gauge pump Shotguns, M-16 rifles, Colt M1911s for sidearms, with helmet, flak jacket, boots, wearing nothing but their underwear. We didn't laugh...out loud.

Looking back upon it all, I find it quite ironic that, perhaps, the greatest season of spiritual development in my life occurred in the context of living on a war machine. We were constantly seeking to deceive, outmaneuver, and overpower our adversaries. At the same time, there was a burgeoning spiritual awakening that was taking place onboard the USS *Saratoga*. Increasingly, my scant spare time not working in Combat Information Center was spent reading my Bible, attending services in the ship's chapel. When in port, I enjoyed hanging out with the growing number of men who identified as Christians and were looking for something to do other than the entertainments and enticements for which sailors are most commonly noted.

Like many young men and women in over the years, I left for military service after high school. Graduating from Independence High School in Charlotte, NC in 1984, my flight to Great Lakes, Illinois in July 1984 was the first time I had ever boarded an airplane. The navy promised travel and adventure and, in my experience, they fulfilled the promise. After Boot Camp at Great Lakes Naval Recruit Training Command, I would spend most of the next six months at OS "A" School, followed by CV Input School (carrier vessel - Input School). These schools prepared me to serve as an Operations Specialist working in the Combat Information Center (CIC) of the USS *Saratoga*.

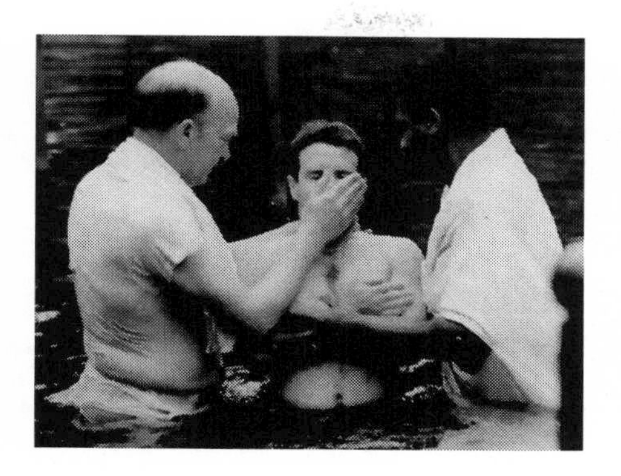

Chaplain Hugo Hammond baptized over 100 enlisted *Saratoga* sailors in Israel's Jordan River. Scripture teaches that baptism symbolizes identification with the death, burial, and resurrection of Jesus Christ. After the initiate is laid back into the water he, or she, is "raised to walk in a new way of life."

My initial expeirence of repentence and faith in Jesus Christ ocurred at a summer camp with my youth group from First Baptist Church Charlotte, NC at Camp Cheerio in Glade Vally, NC in the summer of 1982. My public profession of faith through believer's baptism by immersion would take place later in the Jordan River on November 12, 1985 during our deployment on the *Saratoga*.

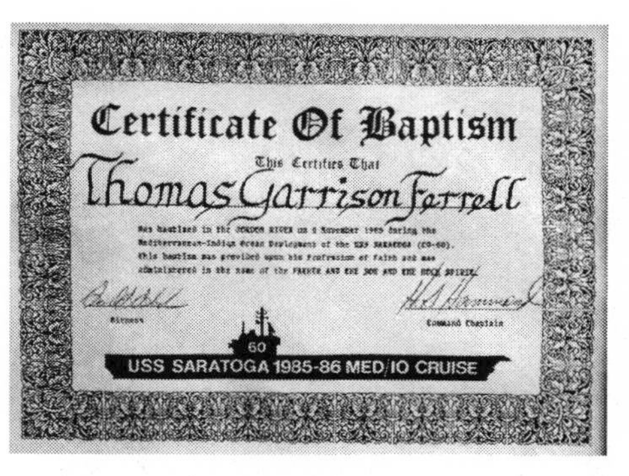

Certificate Of Baptism

This Certifies That

Thomas Garrison Farrell

Was baptized in the JORDAN RIVER on [illegible] November 1985 during the Mediterranean-Indian Ocean Deployment of the USS SARATOGA (CV-60). This baptism was provided upon his profession of faith and was administered in the name of the FATHER AND THE SON AND THE HOLY SPIRIT.

Witness

Command Chaplain

60

USS SARATOGA 1985-86 MED/IO CRUISE

With a combined crew and airwing of 5,000, the *Saratoga* consisted of a ship's company of around 3,000 that was augmented during deployment by our Carrier Air Wing that came from several naval air stations across the country. Our full air wing, of around 2,000 sailors, supported nearly a dozen squadrons indcluding fighter, attack, early-warning, electronic warfare (radar jamming), photo-reconnaissance, airborne refueling, and anti-submarine squadons in helicopter and fixed wing aircraft.

In keeping with longstanding naval traditions, the "Crossing the Line" ceremony, or Shellback Initiation, occurs when a navy ship crosses the equator. It is a fine navy day for those who have been previously initiated, but for those who have not; it is a day that causes many to lose sleep, skin, and the contents of their stomach; not to mention their pride. At the end of the day, when it was all said and done, it seemed to have been great fun for all.

Sanitized Copy Approved for Release 2011/03/04 : CIA-RDP91-00587R000100080005-0

ARTICLE APPEARED ON PAGE

NEWSWEEK
21 October 1985

SPECIAL REPORT

'You Can Run But You Can't Hide'

STAT

The terrorists who hijacked the Achille Lauro fall into an audacious airborne trap.

Sanitized Copy Approved for Release 2011/03/04 : CIA-RDP91-00587R000100080005-0

Saratoga's first international incident on the cruise was the tracking and interception of the Egyptian commercial jet-liner carrying the terrorists who had killed an elderly crippled Jewish-American passenger, Leon Klinghoffer, aboard the high-jacked Italian cruise ship *Achille Lauro*. Seal Team Six would partner with F-14s launched from the *Saratoga* to affect the apprehension of the terrorists. The 1990 movie "Voyage of Terror" cast Burt Lancaster as Mr. Klinghoffer.

My favorite memories of Captain Unruh on the *Saratoga* include his announcements over the 1MC announcing system. His mantra, that all of us could recite, was: "Mighty Fine!" The skipper applied that superlative adjective to many things and the end result was a positive climate that characterized his leadership style. Vice Admiral Unruh even has a boat now by the name of "Mighty Fine." His tenure as skipper on the *Saratoga* included a number of noteworthy accomplishments, including the first-ever night transit of the Suez Canal by an aircraft carrier as well as the first tie-up pier-side by an aircraft carrier at Diego Garcia. In both of these instances, Captain Unruh's experience commanding a deep-draft vessel paid off and he was actively involved in piloting the Saratoga during these challenging occasions.

Shipboard life was filled with routine, but important, things like replenishing food, supplies, and fuel while underway. Pictured above left is the author gazing out to sea and shore, which was a pastime that broke up the monotony for many a sailor. Missile launches, Security Alert drills, and Underway Replenishments served to differentiate the normal at-sea rhythms as the Fire Control technicians, our Marine Detachment (MARDET), and various members of the crew took center stage on these occasions.

More shots of routine operations onboard the *Saratoga* ranging from an underway fueling replenishment to work being done by the Deck Department and the Officers on the Bridge. The bottom left shot is of OS2 John Piccirilli, manning one of the Naval Tactical Data System (NTDS) consoles in CIC. The NTDS was, in fact, the forerunner to the internet that would come about nearly a decade after this picture taken in 1985. Piccirilli was the shipmate whose stand for Christ challenged me to rededicate my life to God. Pictured bottom right are surface and air plot boards in CIC.

The Dallas Cowboys Cheerleaders joining us for a few days in the Indian Ocean was anything but ordinary. As CIC was air-conditioned, America's favorite cheerleaders spent a good few of their waking hours, when not giving shows, in CIC with the OSs. After they left, word on the flight deck was that the guys in laundry had secured the bed sheets upon which our very special guests had slept and these sheets had been manufactured into perfumed strips for sale as souvenirs. The navy was rife with baseless rumors, but this could have actually been true. The facing page shows great liberty shots in Dubrovnik and Singapore. The author is pictured scuba diving in the Caribbean Sea with shipmates on the facing page. (photo credit: EN1 Mike Flint)

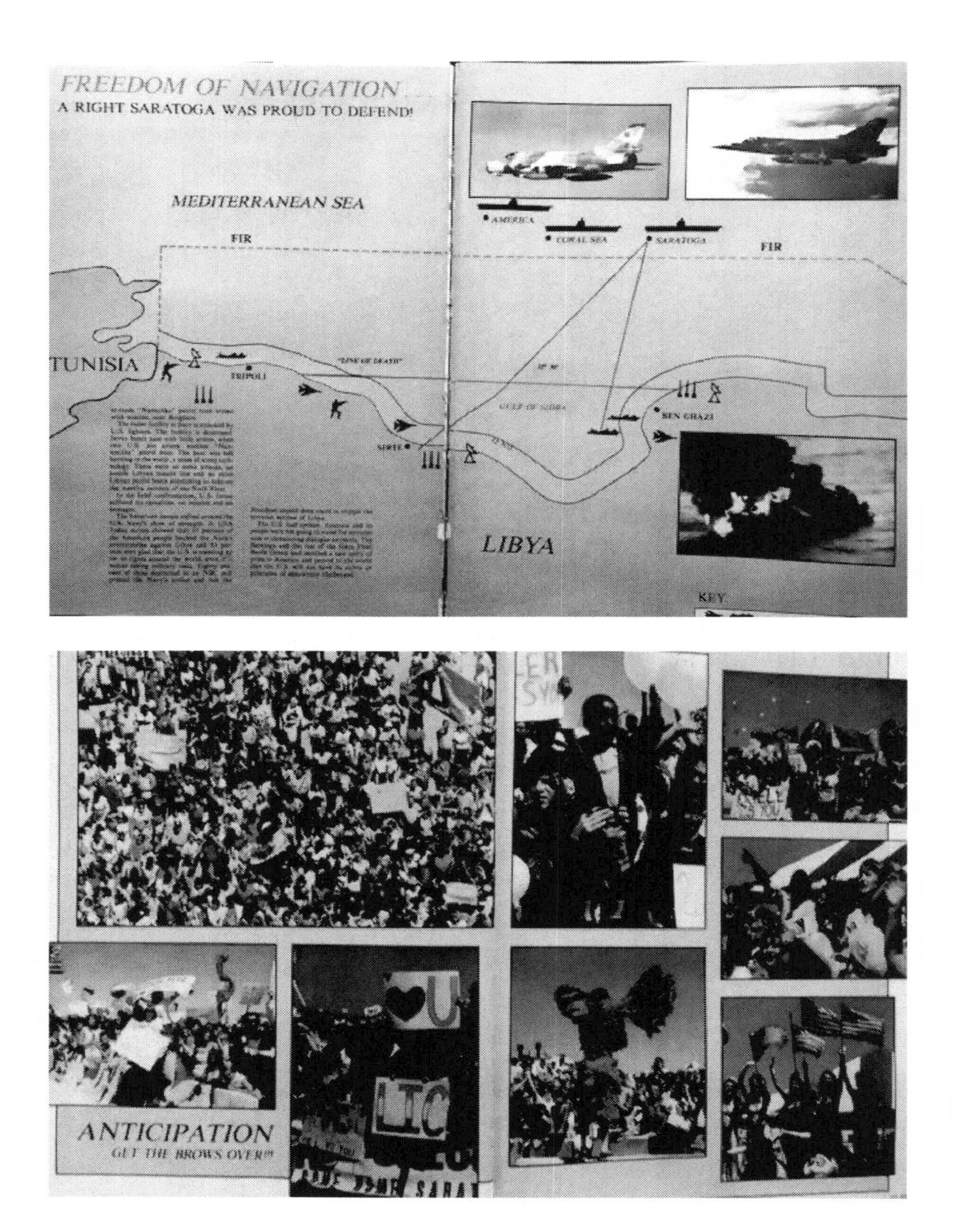

The Homecoming of the *Saratoga* was an enormous celebration at Mayport Naval Station near Jacksonville, Florida. The *Saratoga* had made headlines across the country from the NY Times to the LA Times with the *Achille Lauro* Incident as well as the Libyan Conflict, which was the largest sea battle since World War Two.

Captain Lewis Irving Williams (aka "Gator") served as the Navigator on the USS *Saratoga* during our 1985-86 Med/IO deployment. Being an OS who worked on the Bridge, I was aware that the Gator had been a POW in Viet Nam. In fact, Captain Williams had been shot down in his A-6A over North Viet Nam on 24 April 1967 as a 24-year old naval aviator and he remained in POW status until his release in 1973. Twelve years later, in 1985, Captain Williams would play a significant role in the *Saratoga's* successes as the ship's navigator.
Beyond Captain Williams, a host of other naval officers and senior enlisted men on the Saratoga had begun their naval careers during the Viet Nam era. The men who had served in the Navy during the Viet Nam War were the seasoned and experienced leadership corps of the Navy in the 1980s when the Cold War would finally be won under President Ronald Reagan.

This page is in tribute to all of our Korea and Viet Nam veterans who responded to their country's call to counter the aggressive spread of communism but did not seem to have the full commitment of their government or the full support of their nation. In the Korean War, 33,739 American troops were killed in theatre, 103,284 wounded, and 7,667 are still missing in action. In the Viet Nam War, nearly 60,000 American troops were killed, over 150,000 were wounded, and 1,600 are still missing. Those who came home from these deployments, in many cases, did not receive the welcome that we did on the *Saratoga* upon our return in 1986. God bless these men and women, and I speak for many today who appreciate their sacrifices. Thank-you for your service!

Sending two of my sons off to Georgia College & State University in Milledgeville, Georgia, and observing the contrast between their coming of age years and mine, led me to reflect upon my experiences in the Navy. Our young sailors, soldiers, airmen, and marines give up a lot to serve their countries, and this number includes some who have paid the ultimate price with their lives. On the other side of the equation, military service has been the setting for great opportunity, travel, education, and leadership development in the lives of many young people. I will always be grateful for the experiences I had and the way they contributed to my life after service.

With my wife, Elyse, and sons Garrison, Joseph, and Bailey in Yucatan, Mexico.

What a special day this was at Briarlake Church! We hold outdoor baptismal services several times per year, but on this particular day I had the privilege to baptize former Soviet Army soldier Dobromir Troansky. We were on opposite side during my time on the Saratoga, but now we are brothers in Christ!

Briarlake Baptist Church has over 2,000 members and was chartered in 1959.

Preaching and encouraging churches has marked my life after the *Saratoga.*

Admiral Unruh flew the F-8 Crusader during four Combat tours in Viet Nam, flying 295 missions from the aircraft carrier USS Hancock (CV-19) with VF-24.

Former US Navy Operations Specialist Third Class Petty Officer Tommy Ferrell with Vice-Admiral Jerry Unruh, USN (ret). What an unexpected blessing to reconnect 33 years later! Would you believe that the Admiral has a powerboat named...what else, but the "Mighty Fine!"

CHAPTER 8

AN ALL-VOLUNTEER FORCE

I suppose that everyone who enlists, or takes an officer's commission for that matter, has a unique story to tell. It is also likely that the events and occurrences that add color to that story are, themselves, nearly unforgettable due to the significance of the overall experience of entering military service. Particularly impressionable are the initial steps and early milestones along the way. Eric L. Haney, a founding member of the U.S. Army's Delta Force wrote: "The Military is a profession that brands itself on the soul and causes you forever after to view the world through a unique set of mental filters. The more profound and intense the experience, the hotter the brand, and the deeper it is plunged into you."[16] Because of the uniqueness of military service, it is difficult to grasp, apart from experiencing it, the full weight and emotion one goes through during the process of entry, service, and separation from the military.

My experience started without any initial intent or desire on my part. I was not particularly patriotic, and I was hardly responsible for or dedicated to much beyond myself when I joined the U.S. Navy at the age of 17. It was the summer of 1983 and just after my junior year of high school. Due to a friend of my Dad's named Dave Reule, who went to our church, I landed a pretty good gig as a gopher to a full-time maintenance man employed by the Reule Commercial Realty & Property Management Company in Charlotte, NC. Though the maintenance man with whom I worked was a Navy veteran, this odd coincidence had little to no bearing upon my decision to join the Navy. I do believe, however, that Providence had aligned the whole summer job situation for me.

We were replacing square ceiling tiles in a fairly large two-story commercial building on the busy thoroughfare of East Independence Boulevard when I had my unexpected and unsought after introduction to the world of military service. Part of the building in which we were working was leased to the Navy-Marine Corps Recruiting Office. Uh-oh! The foreshadowing is hard to miss at this point. I discovered that summer that I had little to no natural aptitude for things mechanical, electrical, or anything else that would pertain to a tool-belt. But I quickly became proficient at installing those square ceiling tiles and I had a good natural reach with long arms at around 6 feet tall and probably a smidge or more under 130 lbs. I must also add, in my defense, that I had a good work ethic, boundless energy, and I was in constant demand in our subdivision, Farmwood, for my exceptional grass-cutting skills. I managed both to earn, and squander, a small fortune in those early years. In addition to my work ethic, my parents had taught me to be respectful to adults and I seemed to have a natural way with people.

I don't remember which office - Navy or Marines - that I went into first to replace the ceiling tiles, but it may have been the Marines because I recall the Marine recruiter asking me: "Young Man; how old are you?" "Seventeen," I replied. Jarhead Recruiter: "What do you plan to do after high school?" Sucker reply: "I don't know yet." You can probably imagine how the conversation went from there. Suffice it to say that the Marine Corps recruiter got my name, address, and home phone number.

As it turned out, the Navy was not about to be easily outdone by the Marine Corps. The two branches of service have long been closely intertwined and joined together since 1834, when the Marine Corps Commandant, Archibald Henderson, convinced President Andrew Jackson that the Marines belonged with the Navy rather than the Army, as President Jackson was proposing. Since that time, the Marine Corps has remained a separate branch of the military, but was placed under the Department of the Navy in 1834, where it remains to this day. Many people are surprised to learn that the medics and the chaplains who serve the Marine Corps are drawn from the U.S. Navy. In fact, the Navy also supplies the chaplains for the U.S. Coast Guard as well. All cooperation between the Navy and Marine Corps was put aside, however, when it came to the competitive attempt to recruit a 17-year-old kid who was putting in ceiling tiles with no apparent plans for his future. I went home that day with a bunch of brochures and hardly any more than a fleeting interest in military service with either the Navy or the Marine Corps. However, my personal information had been rendered and a seed must have been planted. It is my recollection that the seed began to sprout on October 23, 1983.

That was the day that the seventeen-year old evidenced his first glimmer of love for country, or something else that I cannot clearly distinguish. On that day, October 23, 1983, two bomb-laden trucks were driven by terrorists into the barracks housing multi-national peacekeeping forces in Beirut, Lebanon. Two hundred forty-one U.S. servicemen, 220 Marines and 21 other U.S military personnel were killed. This was the deadliest single-day body count for the

Marines since the Battle of Iwo Jima in 1945. The FBI said the Beirut truck bombing was the largest non-nuclear blast they had ever observed. Exactly three years later, to the day, on October 23, 1986, at Camp Lejeune in Jacksonville, N.C. a sobering and impressive memorial to the 241 victims of terror would be dedicated. The epithet to these victims of terror reads: "THEY CAME IN PEACE."

The suicide bomber was an Iranian national, and the bombing was later traced to the Hezbollah faction involved in the Lebanese Civil War. It is now an established fact that the Iranians supplied, and still supply, their Shiite Muslim brothers in the Hezbollah (Party of Allah) with weaponry, including bombs and mines to be used against U.S. troops. Former U.S. Ambassador to Lebanon, Jeffrey Feltman, recently wrote that, "Hezbollah is Iran's multi-purpose tool." Ambassador Feltman waxed eloquent saying: "For Iran, Hezbollah is a malevolent version of the Swiss army knife, with special capabilities always at the ready for distinct tasks."[17]

In Hezbollah's slaying of 241 sleeping U.S. peacekeepers in Beirut, the same fractious elements which were influential in my initial interest in joining the military in 1983, would later define my time of service on the USS *Saratoga* during her 1985-86 deployment. The malevolent forces behind the Beirut bombing in 1983, the *Achille Lauro* hijacking in 1985, and the Libyan Conflict of 1986 were the Soviet Union, its regional proxies, and Islamic terrorism such as Hezbollah. In short, the bombing in Beirut on October 23, 1983 was the match that lit the powder under me. It seemed to me, even at the young age of 17, like a cowardly and hostile act of terror against honorable representatives of our nation.

"Well now they have gone and done it! Dad gum it! I'm going to join the Marines!" That's what I said, but at 17 you can't legally join the U.S. military without a parent's signature. The fact that I had evidenced no particular ambition for a college education did not go unnoticed by my parents. My dad was a banking clerical accountant and my mother was an elementary school teacher. In fact, my mother would later say, repeatedly, that she had told the principal of Independence High School that he had no business letting me graduate as I had done nothing to deserve the honor. My response to her awkward assertion of educational apathy on my part was a blank stare and the sound of crickets chirping in the background. If I'm not mistaken, she actually gave the principal that exact speech just minutes after he had handed me my high school diploma.

Beyond her lack of enthusiasm for my academic efforts, my mother was not well adjusted to the thought of her only son leaving for military service, particularly during a time of increasing hostility towards American forces stationed overseas. Suffice it to say that my mom would not sign for the Marine Corps after the high death toll bombing of the Marine Barracks in Beirut. However, the combination of the effective wooing of the Navy recruiter and my interest in overseas travel, as the Navy effectively glamorized it, won the day. I enlisted in the U.S. Navy, with parental permission, through the Delayed Entry Program (DEP) at the age of 17, sometime before Christmas of 1983.

The Armed Services Vocational Aptitude Battery Test (ASVAB) must be a telltale indicator because my lack of skills with a toolbelt put me into two possible slots. The Naval Career Counsellor wanted me to take the Nuclear Engineering Aptitude Exam to ascertain my viability for nuclear engineering work on a nuclear sub or a nuclear-powered aircraft carrier. I laughed and told him I hated math. Turns out the Navy doesn't take no for an answer. I was whisked away in a conspicuous car with government plates to an undisclosed location in Charlotte to undergo "nuclear testing" or something like that. Suffice it to say, after my return from the nuke test, they showed no further interest in sending me to the Navy's Nuclear Engineering School in Charleston, SC.

The detailer looked over my file, including ASVAB Test, and told me about the Navy's 17-week "Operations Specialist 'A' School" at Dam Neck Fleet Combat Training Center in Dam Neck, Virginia. It sounded pretty cool and he assured me that I could segue from there to BUD/S (Basic Underwater Demolition/Seal) School in Coronado, California. The OS rating, at that time, was one of the vocational streams into the Naval Special Warfare program, specifically, the Navy SEALS (so named due to the environments in which they are equipped to operate – sea, air, & land).

Since the war on terror commenced on September 11, 2001, the Navy added a specific rating called Special Warfare Operator so that the SEALS no longer tend to come from several other rating streams as they did in my day, but instead they now have their own expedited and dedicated rating pipeline into the Naval Special Warfare Program. The SEAL trainees spend a minimum of 21 weeks in BUDS School after completing Naval Boot Camp and a three-week BUDS orientation. From there, they go on to further training before earning the coveted Trident pin, which marks the members of the SEAL Teams.

The public did not know much about Navy SEALS in those days when I enlisted, and the SEALS had only recently been formed in 1962 by President John F. Kennedy. The predecessor unit to the SEALS were the Naval Combat Demolition Units of WWII, and the Underwater Demolition Teams (UDTs), thereafter. Since the mid-1980s the public awareness of the Navy SEALS has dramatically increased. Along with the more visible role that the SEALS have taken addressing the increasing number of terrorist attacks since the late 1980s, there has been no shortage of movies, television documentaries, books, and even a TV series, popularizing their exploits. I had only learned of them in late October of 1983, when my Navy recruiter revealed their presence to me in order to direct my interest away from joining the Marine Corps.

As I was told by the recruiter and the detailer who slotted me for OS "A" School, there would be opportunities for those who are interested in the SEAL program to take the initial physical fitness assessment in Boot Camp so as to receive orders to BUD/S after OS "A" School. Sadly, on the day of the BUD/S fitness assessment at boot camp our Company Commander, Chief Bussell, was disgruntled over our company's excessive stupidity for some reason that escapes me. As a result, we were locked down with no privileges permitted whatsoever.

I missed the opportunity to take the SEAL Fitness Exam. There wouldn't be another. But the thought of going to Coronado for BUD/S School was ever on my mind. I would run long distances and swim far out in the frigid Atlantic Ocean off the shores of Dam Neck in OS "A" School in October and November 1985 with a classmate named Flynn who had gotten orders after the Fitness Test in boot camp for BUDS; contingent upon his completion of OS "A" School. By the way, Flynn would graduate first in our class and I have often wondered how things went for him at Coronado. I suspect that he finished and earned his Trident. He was a sharp dude.

But before all of that, on Saturday July 14, 1985, I would officially step off the long white bus with U.S. government plates that shuttled a rag tag looking bunch of young males of differing color, size, and motivation level from Chicago's O'Hare Airport to the Naval Training Command at Great Lakes. I say "rag-tag" because that is exactly how I felt after the "hurry up and wait" routine of the past two days while waiting around the MEPS (Military Entrance Processing Station) compounded by delays, including flight delays to Chicago's O'Hare. Anybody who has served in the military understands the phenomenon of "hurry up and wait," which often characterized my time in the service. I also say "rag-tag" because the other guys stepping off of that bus who had flown to Chicago from all over the United States, plus our territories, looked really disheveled. If they had been through what I had been through, then such appearances were excusable. Undoubtedly, most of them had spent the last night, or two, partying *Like it's 1999* as PRINCE had melodiously boasted in the hit song released in 1982.

On the long day that I left for boot camp, my dad had driven me to MEPS on his way to work at the First Union National Bank in downtown Charlotte. Looking back, I guess my mom had not been able to handle the emotion of it. She was a schoolteacher and it was July so she could have gone. Undoubtedly, my mom would have gone, but it must have been too difficult for her emotionally. The task fell to my dad, as it should have. Dad always went to work early to beat the traffic. MEPS was on the way for him. Dropping me off was difficult on us both. I don't remember much more than that except that I'd forgotten the banana that I had brought along for breakfast. I must have left it on the front seat of his truck. The truck that I had previously wrecked...twice.

Because we were in the downtown area in morning commute time and traffic was heavy, I exited the truck swiftly. I grabbed my few permitted items in my gym bag, and hugged my dad. This was getting real! I am not at all sure to what extent it may have dawned on me that I was trailing off, albeit awkwardly and without my banana, on a fast-paced journey to manhood. In fact, that journey would swiftly commence in less than five minutes when the shouting began regarding what to do next: where to stand, when to breath, you get the idea. Probably, twenty long minutes had passed. Suddenly, from nowhere, there stood my father. He was dressed in his coat and tie for work, but looking conspicuously sad. In his uplifted hand he held a banana: "You forgot this, son." Apparently good ole Dad had discovered my banana in the truck when he reached the bank. He made the trip back through morning rush-hour traffic to MEPS, just to bring it to me. At least that is what he said. Even then, with my teenage male insensitivity, I sensed that this was about more than just a banana. Dad hugged me again and I was suddenly struck by the emotion of the moment. I don't remember if any tears were shed but I can tell you that I'm crying while typing this thirty-five years later. With both parents now dearly departed, such memories are now more evocative of raw emotion than I recall having at the time.

One of the greatest things about being a Christian is the certainty with which we know that we will live eternally, and we will see again the loved ones with whom we will spend eternity. In such moments of sober reflection, I take great comfort from the words of the Apostle Paul, who said: "to be absent from the body is to be present with the Lord." He also said that "we do not grieve as those who have no hope." I often reflect upon those promises from God's Word.

Thirty-five years have passed since Dad gave me that banana and saw me off to join the Navy on July 14, 1984. He left me for heaven on December 29, 1994, dying of prostate cancer at the age of 60, while I was in seminary. During that ten-year period after my enlistment ended and before my father died, he told me on many occasions how proud he was of me. It is difficult to put into words what a wonderful feeling it is to know that your father is proud of you and that he also tells others of his pride.

For example, one of Dad's life-long friends from the First Baptist Church of Charlotte, Joe Caudell, used to get a big kick out of embellishing my father's accounts of what the *Saratoga* was doing during our deployment, as it was "supposedly" relayed to him by my Dad. Dad's source of all information in those days was the print media contained in the *Charlotte Observer* (a morning publication), the *Charlotte News* (an afternoon publication which ceased in 1985), and *Time Magazine*; all of which he read cover to cover.

I know that my dad followed meticulously the press coverage of the *Saratoga*'s exploits on our Med/IO Cruise and, according to family friend Joe Caudell, my Dad may have embellished my role in the well-publicized circumstances of our deployment. After I returned home following the cruise, Joe would go on waxing eloquent as he had developed quite a monologue about how I had ascended the Crow's Nest of the *Saratoga* and single-handedly taken out ships, subs, planes, trains and automobiles. Never mind that we didn't even have a "Crow's Nest." Probably, my Dad just tried to explain what we did in CIC, on the Bridge, and as lookouts above the Bridge, and Joe took it from there. But the comforting thing, after these many years, is that my Mom and Dad were proud of me and my life was changing for the better since my time on the *Saratoga*.

Ever since my conversion to Christ at the age of sixteen at Camp Cheerio in the summer of 1982, I had an up and down experience with regard to the consistency of my walk with Jesus Christ. Bad habits that had taken root before my conversion such as partying with friends, alcohol, marijuana use, random acts of stupidity, and general waywardness would ebb and flow depending upon my proximity to church, the youth group and, more importantly, to God Himself. Looking back on it, I would have to say that I was more "off" than "on" in terms of living the Christian life with integrity and faithfulness.

Like my enlistment in the Navy, my walk with the LORD really boiled down to a deliberate willingness to volunteer myself to a higher purpose. The difference was that once in the Navy, you are in. In the Christian life, you can never loose your relationship with God, as the Scripture says that you have been adopted into God's family and sealed by His Holy Spirit.[18] You can, however, walk away from fellowship with God and sadly, I did walk away from God for most of my high school years, even after my conversion.

Really, I was struggling to find my place in the largest high school in North Carolina at the time. I had always been very outgoing and popular from my earliest years through middle school. Girls had always like me and I liked it that they liked me. At Northeast Junior High I was even voted Valentine King by my peers in my 9th grade year, whatever that meant. Though without great skills or much playing time, but due to determination and tenacity, I had made the varsity football team which went undefeated, won our division championship, and I was a member of the Monogram Club. But I wasn't satisfied with that and seemed to long for something more exciting and exhilarating.

I mentioned earlier the all-night hang outs that my best friend Brian and I pulled by telling our moms that we were spending the night at each other's house. We took advantage of their gullibility by going to unchaperoned parties until late at night and by walking around Mint Hill through the early hours of the morning, trying not to freeze to death. Adventure seemed to be in my blood. Partying at the rock quarry, daring dives and goofy jumps off of high cliffs into deep waters forty feet below, followed by long swims across large bodies of deep open water were some of our routine escapades. Driving cars dangerously with several wrecks to show for it hardly even seemed to give me pause.

All the while I was living in the moment, wasting my time academically, and drifting further from the high social standing that I had enjoyed during my previous years in junior high school. Added to all of that drama was my transition into young adulthood. I was slow to arrive at puberty, yet tall and skinny, very skinny. I was always tough as nails, scrappy, and willing to fight. Since I was skinny, some larger peers assumed I was one to be trifled with, but I was not. Sadly, now, I admit that I had gained some experience in fighting during junior and senior high.

A couple of anecdotes to paint the picture of the vulnerabilities so characteristic of my youthful existence before I got it together on the *Saratoga* may be worthwhile. I remember clearly the inspections that we were subjected to on a daily basis in boot camp. Chief Bussell, our Senior Company Commander previously mentioned in conjunction with his amazing ability to call marching cadence, was a combination of police officer, football coach, father, and schoolteacher to us young recruits. After the first introduction to him at 0400 on my first day waking up in Navy Boot Camp it is surprising that I was able to get past my initial abject fear of the man. But, for sure, that first morning was AWFUL!

About eighty of us were making a very abrupt transition from civilian to military life. We were been consolidated into one unit as company 219. We had all gotten off one of the several buses arriving at the gate of Naval Recruit Training Command (RTC) Great Lakes from O'Hare Airport. Then, we were pushed through a predictable routine of paper signing and lectures laced with profanity, the likes of which even I was not used to hearing.

Around midnight of our arrival day at RTC, we were still in civilian clothes (civies) and sporting long uncut hair when we got to bed. Like the barracks to which Company 219 would soon be assigned, the processing barracks had two long rows of twenty sets of bunkbeds in each row. The two rows of bunkbeds faced one another with maybe ten yards separating the two long rows of bunkbeds. The bunkbeds, themselves, were maybe five yards from one another in each of the two rows. The space between the two facing rows would become the torture chamber where we were punished for many things, and anything, by our Company Commanders. The CCs would often make us drop for push-ups and flutter kicks. You would literally get out of your bunk and commence to push-ups on most mornings. Fortunately, for me, the physical part of boot camp was not very challenging. The mental head games, on the other hand, were sometimes hard to endure.

By midnight, after a long draining day in unfamiliar and menacing surroundings, those thin mattresses with tightly wrapped military style sheets and a grey wool blanket were certainly good enough for us. Then at 4am, or 0400, it happened! The fluorescent lights were suddenly thrown on with full wattage and a wiry black man of average height dressed in military khakis was screaming foul language at us as we awoke from our brief slumber. I'm not sure which loud horrid sound came first? Was it the steel trash can hurled down the aisle between the two rows of bunkbeds by the man in khakis cussing like he had just stumped his toe for the second time, or was it the cussing and yelling that awakened us. Like the chicken and the egg; we may never know.

Since I distinctly remember the sight of the trash can clanging and bouncing down the center aisle early that morning, I realized Chief Bussell must have turned the lights on first, then starting yelling and cursing at us. Then, from somewhere must have come the idea to pick up the heavy steel trash can with both hands, lift it fully above his head and throw it with all his might down that long center aisle. I won't repeat what he said after that but suffice it to say that I've never forgotten it. I did tell my teenage boys what the Chief said once, and they thought it was very "hardcore" and seemed embarrassed. So you know it must have been pretty bad.

Well....at least we had gotten to know our company commander. Actually, when compared with that first encounter, everything that would follow for the next nine weeks would seem pretty mild by comparison. The Chief was actually pretty cool by the end of boot camp. But I do remember, one time when under inspection the Chief noticed some "peach-fuzz," as he called it, on my chin. The truth was, that as a brand new eighteen-year old, I still didn't even need to shave, and I certainly didn't have any practice at the art. As I mentioned earlier, puberty came later for me than most, and that was part of the self-consciousness I felt in high school in addition to being pretty thin.

Leave it to the sadistic nature of a company commander to devise an appropriate solution to the "peach-fuzz" and every other problem we caused for him. Upon noticing, maybe three tiny and fine chin hairs, Chief Bussell quickly pulled out a cigarette lighter in the front pocket of his khaki pants, flicked it, and used its flame to burn the "peach fuzz" right off of my chin. I really do think Chief Bussell liked me, and between us, we had no further problems after the lighter incident as I recall.

I should also add that boot camp developed the religious impulses of young men in general, at least that was the case in Company 219. Besides regular chapel services on Sundays attended by many of us in boot camp in those days, I recall that someone among the 80 or so recruits of Company 219 would typically say a good night prayer just after taps as we were going to bed. It was a very democratic phenomenon, as there were really no standout spiritual leaders in our company at that time. Whoever felt led to pray would just pray before we went to sleep. I really wish I had that on video now. It would be interesting to watch. It just seemed that the stress of it all drove us sincerely to prayer. It must be something to do with the old adage that there are no atheists in foxholes.

If the peach-fuzz story illustrates that I was a bit behind my peers in physical maturity, an occurrence during OS "A" School at the Enlisted Club affirms that I did not lack the courage to respond to threats. This tendency to respond quickly with action has characterized me from my earliest days. Again, before I found resolution to my walk with Christ, my spiritual life was really up and down from the age of 16 to nearly 19.

One night, I made my way...for after-hours food and entertainment. As I was preparing to exit the club to walk back to the barracks, another young OS who was in my school, but not my class, was coming into the club and for some reason, perhaps he was drunk, he spit on my shoes. Not one to turn the other cheek at that season of my life, I called him out in disrespectful terms. He countered with similar language, after which we agreed to go outside for conflict resolution.

Ever since I had survived a bully situation at the initiative of an aggressive senior wrestler when I was in the eleventh grade, I began taking martial arts. Actually, I'd survived the after-school altercation through the means of a well-placed right hook, the additional firepower of my newly arrived class ring, and the good fortune of a nearby adult to break up the fight pretty quickly, that left me the undisputed winner before the odds changed. To best an upperclassman who was an accomplished high school wrestler was no small achievement on my part. But in order to hedge any future bets, I began taking Martial Arts at the Kim School of Tae Kwon Do on East

Independence Boulevard and continued throughout my senior year. The fight outside of the Drifting Dirt was the first actual application of my training beyond sparring. Once the antagonist approached me outside the club, I quickly responded with a reverse punch technique to the nose that had been practiced for over a year.

Even I was surprised at how well that thing worked. I guess you could say I got my money's worth from 8th degree black belt Instructor Ju Huhn Kim. Suddenly, the other guy was on the ground with a lot of blood everywhere. I quickly ascertained that it was in my best interest to vacate the scene, but apparently that did not happen quickly enough. The military police tracked me across the base in their golf cart through the dark of night before I could even make it back to my barracks. I was busted.

I was taken down to the brig and informed that the other guy had been taken to the base hospital. I could see that my Navy career had taken a bad turn. Cited with Uniform Code of Military Justice violations and scheduled for Captain's Mast, I was suddenly in a pretty bad situation. It didn't help that I remembered from the naval history we learned in boot camp that the term "Captain's Mast," was a loaded term with serious implications. The term, Captain's Mast, dated back to old seagoing days when offenders of various sorts were tied to the mast of the ship after being sentenced by the Captain. There they would receive the appropriate number of lashes from the whip for their infractions. I knew that was all old school, but I was worried about the outcome of my pending Captain's Mast none the less.

CHAPTER 9

GENERAL QUARTER – THIS IS NOT A DRILL

When I received my orders for the *Saratoga*, upon graduation from OS "A" School, the unfortunate instance of my fight with another operations specialist in training just outside the Shifting Sands Enlisted Club on Base at Dam Neck was over two months behind me. The fight had taken place sometime between my arrival to "A" School in mid-September 1984 but before Christmas of the same year. I was probably around halfway through the 17 weeks of "A" School when it occurred. Both of the guilty parties were cited for Article 117 of the Uniform Code of Military Justice, as I recall, which says: "Any person subject to this chapter who uses provoking or reproachful words or gestures towards any other person subject to this chapter shall be punished as a court-martial may direct."

In truth, we could have been charged with fighting which had greater stigma and penalty. All in all, things could have been worse. I had definitely gained the respect of my peers, including the fellow with whom I had been in the brief altercation. I ran into him at a Navy party in a hotel room at Virginia Beach some weeks after the fight. His lip was still fat with stitches, but we were all friendly with no further issues remaining. I remember being sought out for weekend excursions into Virginia Beach by classmates due to the aforementioned climate of hostility in town towards military personnel in uniform. Strangely, I recall a classmate named Paul, who said, in typical Navy jargon: "Hey, if we get in some shit with the locals, at least we can count on Ferrell." I recall being gratified by this expression of affirmation, and it is strange that I still remember "Paul" by his first name. In the service, everyone pretty much goes by last names and this practice is first instilled in Boot Camp, where Company Commanders yell at you using your last name. Rarely did one even know another's first name in my experience in military service. It seems strange in retrospect, but that is just the way it was.

But for some odd reason, I recall Paul by his first name and still remember the new found esteem among my classmates after the fight at the Shifting Sands that night. Though I was facing Captain's Mast, I had proven to my classmates that I would back up my talk, and I was not one to run from a fight. Such respect goes a long way in the military, especially among foolish young men, as most of us were at that time.

Nevertheless, my mom and dad were concerned when I told them what had happened and that I had a captain's mast pending. I was really trying to straighten up and had not even been drinking at the Drifting Dirt that night. But I was in the wrong place at the wrong time, and my feet still seemed directed towards places that were not in my best interest, particularly as a young unseasoned follower of Jesus Christ. Shifting Sands, the base club, even advertised strippers that came on certain occasions. I doubt that such things are permitted in the 21st century military on official bases, but I am not sure. I remember a particular occasion when I had duty as a Gate Security Guard at the entrance to the base at Dam Neck. Every OS in training had to pull certain watch duty assignments, and typically such duty involved standing security at the front gate of the base.

One day I was standing watch and a young civilian woman, maybe in her mid-twenties, approached the gate and said that she was supposed to be entertaining at the Shifting Sands. She produced her I.D. and an official promotional flier which verified the presence of strippers at the club as well as her involvement in the affair. A male about her age was also with her, and I remember thinking that it must be sad for him to accompany his apparent wife or girlfriend into such an environment for such an occasion. My Christian upbringing, even before I was a Christian, had always seasoned me to respect the opposite sex, and I instinctively knew that sexual activity was a serious matter.

I avoided, sometimes by the intervention of Providence, sexual misconduct and held women in high regard. As I had mentioned earlier, my transition from 9th grade Valentine King in junior high to rarely dating in High School was a fact of life that helped to keep me from some of the facts of life. In truth, most of the girls I was frequently around as my life was degenerating into the party scene would not have been good for my soul, and I seemed to know that. On one occasion, I was to meet a girl after midnight for less than noble purposes, and she was involved in a wreck on the way to the rendezvous. It seemed that the good Lord was always protecting me from some of the more ensnaring habits to which I was naturally gravitating.

Another occasion I recall while standing guard at the front gate was the day a long haired and whiskered white male in his mid-twenties wearing blue jeans and a t-shirt approached the gate and produced a military I.D. card which bore his name and showed his rank to be E-5 (Petty Officer Second Class). Well, I can tell you that some long-haired freak with a fake military ID card was not about to get past me that day. I detained him, and he politely asked to see my watch supervisor, who was full-time military police (or Master at Arms). The hippie and my watch supervisor spoke in conference inside the Guard Station for a minute or two at which point my supervisor placed a call, and the matter was apparently resolved. Both the watch supervisor and the long-haired Petty Officer Second Class came back to the place where I was standing, and my supervisor said that the Petty Officer was to gain entrance. He explained that this man had "relaxed grooming standards." I apologized to the hairy sailor and he respectfully said: "No problem, shipmate, you were just doing your job."

I wouldn't understand the nature of that occasion at the front gate or the purpose of "relaxed grooming standards" until a few weeks later. I often swam at the outstanding Aquatic Facility that had been recently built and was housed in a remote section of the base at Dam Neck. There were diving platforms of various heights, including some unusually high ones, underwater observation windows onlooking the pool, and the place was just amazing. For a guy who liked to swim, this was as good as it gets indoors. I swam often in the open ocean and the aquatic center, and I still aspired to getting orders to BUD/S after OS "A" School to become a Navy SEALS. Running and swimming with my OS classmate Flynn, who had orders to BUD/S after OS "A" School, made the possibility seem all the more tangible.

On one occasion, I went with several of my classmates to the Base Aquatic Center. Upon arrival, we were stopped outside and told that the pool was closed, but opening soon. We had to wait, and I am glad that we stood outside and waited because we were treated to the sight of a couple of dozen of the toughest looking guys that I had ever seen, and all with "relaxed grooming standards". They were coming out of the Aquatic Center with large dive bags and lots of amazing black tactical gear and military hardware. At that time, in 1985, Navy SEALS Team Six, or Special Development Group (DEVGRU), was virtually unknown as the Navy's Tier-1 Counterterrorism and Hostage Rescue Response Team. In fact, Seal Team Six had just been formed a few years previous following the Iran hostage-rescue debacle, referred to as Operation Eagle-Claw, had met with failure back in 1980.

A Vietnam-era Seal, Richard Marcinko had already commanded Seal Team Two, when he was tasked with the start-up of Seal Team Six in 1981. He chose the designation 6 because the Navy only had two Seal Teams at the time: Seal Team One was at Coronado on the West Coast and Seal Team Two was based on the east coast at nearby Little Creek Amphibious Naval Base. In the spirit of Sun Tzu's words on the importance of deception in military victories, Marcinko wanted the Soviets to think that there were six Seal Teams instead of only three. Actually, by 1984, Marcinko had just relinquished command of Seal Team Six and taken on a new assignment from the top Navy brass. His new duty was to begin operating "Red Cell," another naval special operations group founded for the purpose of testing the security of select mission critical military bases around the world in the rising age of terroristic threats.

As both Seal Team Six and Red Cell had Dam Neck for home base, it is certain that we ran into one or the other of these two groups, or maybe some from both teams, on that interesting day at the pool. My OS classmates were doing a double take on the long-haired guys, who looked as though they could have been the U.S.

Scuba Diving Olympic Team, coming out of the Aquatic Center all geared up that day. I looked on knowingly and pointed respectfully, saying, "Relaxed Grooming Standards." Undoubtedly, all of us, including Flynn, were impressed. We had not been that close to the Navy's elite warriors in the line of duty since doing swim training and water survival training back in boot camp. This encounter was different. The Seals walking around the pool instructing recruits at Great Lakes seemed laid back in comparison to these mighty warriors who were dubbed the elite of the elite. Dam Neck still serves as the Home Base for DEVGRU (aka Seal Team Six) to this day. OS "A" School was recently moved back to Great Lakes Naval Station in Great Lakes, IL where it was prior to moving to Dam Neck, when I attended the school. I don't think the present OS's in Great Lakes will likely be bumping into Seal Team Six as we did back in the day.

When I reported to the USS *Saratoga* (CV-60) in late March of 1985, I had finished 9 weeks of boot camp (including one week of initial processing), 17 weeks of OS "A" School, and 4 additional weeks of CV-Input school to prepare me specifically for working in the CIC of an aircraft carrier. I was already three quarters through my first year of a three-year active duty enlistment (three years of reserve duty would follow) and I had been in school for the whole time. That was about to change. By march of 1985, I was still only 18 years old; yet with my initial training all completed, it was time to report to the fleet for sea duty. Generally, I recall being excited, but I knew that I had much to learn, and that military environments can be pretty hard on the new guy.

Many tricks are played upon newbies to the fleet, but the Navy has a way of preparing you not to be overly gullible. That preparation comes in boot camp where ridiculous rumors are circulated, perhaps intentionally by the company commanders, in order to instill a spirit of scrutiny and dispel gullibility. In boot camp, for example, we heard that the rock bank Van Halen had died in an airplane crash. That was bull. We were also told that in the upcoming "Shot Day" we would receive all of the inoculations that we would need for the fleet and any travel contingency. This much was true. We were told that we would line up with our t-shirt sleeves rolled up and proceed in single file down a gauntlet line receiving the inoculations in rapid fire. So far...true. We were also told by the company commanders, with straight face, that we had only one shot that would be a problem for us. That was the square needle in the left testicle. Yes...we would be receiving a shot with a square needle in the left testicle. Now that one sounded very bad.

It seems silly now, but with all the stress they had put us through, and it being just the second week of mental torment in boot camp, we must have been at a vulnerable state to believe that story. But we did: hook, line, and sinker. Maybe it was the unfamiliarity of the environment. Maybe all of the engineered stress to which we were subjected, but I had never heard more weird talk from people who were asleep than I heard during those first weeks of boot camp. I remember one guy, McCreary, who sat straight up in his rack while asleep and shouted loudly, "Attention on Deck," just as we had to do when our Company Commander, or any boot camp Company Commander with a red shoulder tassel, walked into any room which we occupied.

This "Attention on Deck" thing probably happened fifty times on any given day at least. Often times, you would be dropped for push-ups or flutter kicks following the drill of "Attention on Deck." If not told to drop, you were to remain rigidly at attention hoping that your mere presence did not trigger the said person to whom you were giving honor by standing. When said person, after his entry, was sufficiently satisfied, then he would disdainfully say,

"Carry On." Then, it was in the script for us to reply, "Aye-Aye Sir!" Then we went about whatever our business was before the interruption until the next one occurred.

In the case of McCreary sitting up in his rack and talking in his sleep, he shouted out the whole sequence: "Attention on Deck!" "Carry On!" Then he said: "Aye-Aye Sir" to himself before falling straight back into his rack all from the sitting up position. As I was on watch by myself when all of this happened, patrolling the barracks with an old M-1 Garand Rifle, which we carried while marching, I had no one to laugh with on that occasion. I may have entered it into the watch logbook, but probably not. I now wish I had. It would be a viral video for sure.

So, after believing stupid things which were told in boot camp, some about our own demise, we slowly were conditioned not to worry about stuff and to doubt rumors in general. That being the case, I don't recall falling for many freshman tricks on the "Boat," as the crew called the *Saratoga*, nor was I very worried about the change of environment. But suddenly being thrown in with many older guys who had been in the Navy for a while has a humbling effect on a newbie to the fleet. The old coping strategy of boot camp, just stay below the radar and don't get noticed, seemed to be the wise approach on the ship. But, unfortunately, I had a Captain's Mast blemish on my record, due to the fight I had gotten into at the base club, and that with less than a year of time in service. As a result of my early enlistment through the Delayed Entry Program, my rank would have been E-3 by this time. But as a consequence of the fight at the Base Club, I had been busted down to E-2.. More importantly, my Division Leadership in the OI Division was tipped off that I had caused sufficient trouble in OS "A" School to warrant a Captain's Mast, albeit with a pretty light sentence.

I don't think I had been on the ship two weeks when I overheard a conversation that would serve as a dramatic catalyst for change in my life. The *Saratoga* was tied up pier-side in our homeport of Mayport, Florida undergoing a typical pre-deployment pattern involving short week-long stints at sea, usually in the nearby Jacksonville Operating Area, followed by short periods back at home of another week or two. Most of the younger and single enlisted guys held residence on the ship even when we were in port, while married guys, and all of the officers, lived off the ship on base, or in nearby civilian housing. I was hanging out in the TV lounge adjacent to the OI Division berthing compartment (where all of the OSs E-6 and below slept underway and many of the younger guys also berthed while in port). It was in the TV Lounge that I overheard several of the OSs interrogating a guy, OS3 Picarilli, about whether or not he planned to go drinking with them anymore. They were putting pressure on him to continue in the party lifestyle and they were calling attention to his new-found "religion."

Being a brand-new guy on the ship, only 18 years of age, and an inconsistent middle of the road Christian, I just kept my mouth shut. Meanwhile, these fellow OS's were intently questioning this new Christian, Picarilli, about his faith. I watched with curious interest and, more importantly, I came under great conviction as he faithfully explained how he had given his life to Christ at a nearby church last week and that he was trying to make some lifestyle changes. He explained that he was still their friend and he still wanted to hang out with them, but that he did feel like a different person in some ways that might be difficult for them to understand. They seemed satisfied for the moment that they had not lost a friend, and I went back to my rack later that evening to consider what had transpired before me.

Over the course of that sleepless night, I thought about my own conversion to Christ at the age of 16 back at Camp Cheerio in the summer of '82. In my mind the tape played of my up and down Christian walk over the past several years. During my senior year of high school, my Youth Minister, Don Brock, had asked me to be the Pastor for Youth Week, which occurred in the Spring every year. During that week, different students who were all seniors in high school, would take the place of the church staff members at First Baptist Charlotte. Somebody was assigned to be the Children's Minister, the Youth Minister, the Music Minister, the Pastor, and other church personnel. As the Pastor, I was expected to give a 15-minute sermon in our Sunday night service at the church, which was televised on a local cable channel in Charlotte.

From the time of junior high school, I did not even like reading aloud in front of others. I would get terribly nervous, even panicky, when I was called to read the Bible in the Sunday evening Church Training Union classes which Southern Baptist Churches held in those days. I'm not sure why I was so self-conscious in junior high because I had always been a good reader. To read in front of others, or to pray publicly in church, for that matter, caused me great anxiety. I remember wanting to talk with my parents about it, but I was too ashamed. My conversion to Christ would set me on a path that would ultimately lead me to the pulpit as a pastor speaking to hundreds, even thousands, on regular and various occasions, but nothing was further from my mind, not even by my senior year, when Don asked me to be the Pastor at Youth Week.

I am still surprised to this day that I was asked to be the pastor. Another young man seemed infinitely more qualified, particularly in comparison with me. Brian Bailey was a sharp young man in our church who boarded at the NC School of Science and Mathematics in Durham, North Carolina, and he had just been awarded a Morehead Scholarship to attend the University of North Carolina at Chapel Hill. The fact that he had been away for most of the past few two years in boarding school probably accounted for his occupation of the role of Associate Pastor; while I was given the heavy lifting that came with the role of Senior Pastor. Both of us were actually allotted the same speaking time, 15 minutes each for our sermons, and I would follow the Associate Pastor. Even I had the sense to notice that I was outgunned.

In just a few months, while I was in Navy boot camp at Great Lakes, Brian would attend the University of North Carolina on a Morehead Scholarship, serve there as President of the Student Body, get a Stanford MBA, and later serve in the Clinton White House under Deputy Chief of Staff Erskine Bowles, before working at the Carlyle Group, a global investment firm. When Don told me that I was to follow Brian Bailey, I must have thought: "Why don't I just sit this one out? I've been church friends with Brian since we were in the church nursery, I think he's got this." I was clearly apprehensive, even anxious, about my upcoming preaching obligation in the pulpit of the First Baptist Church of Charlotte, and I had to follow Brian Bailey.

And yet I couldn't seem to shake this divine calling that seemed to be pursuing me. God was arranging things in my life from my salvation experience at Camp Cheerio at the age of 16 to a summer job one year later putting in ceiling tiles in the Navy Recruiting Building on East Independence Boulevard, to being the apprehensive pastor at Youth Week just weeks before high school graduation and my departure to Great Lakes for boot camp. After that would come OS "A" School, Carrier Vessel Input Training and then on to the USS *Saratoga* in late March of 1985 for the life changing cruise that would change everything for me. Looking back upon it all instills within me a tremendous sense of gratitude, awe, and wonder for a God who is so personal and forgiving, even when I was an inconsistent follower at best.

I remember feeling impressed to preach upon a biblical text that stunned me, where Jesus was in the Garden of Gethsemane the night he would be betrayed and then crucified on the following day. He prayed to his Heavenly Father with great anxiety, even sweating great drops of blood.[19] In fact, the sweat glands in the forehead are surrounded by tiny blood vessels which constrict and dilate, especially when under great pressure. These tiny blood vessels can rupture under severe pressure and cause the blood to effuse through the sweat glands. This rare condition is called "hematidrosis." As a young Christian, I was struck that Jesus, God's promised Messiah and Savior, was willing to go to the cross and die as a substitute for my sins. From the vantage point of a comprehensive survey of the Jewish law, the writer of Hebrews said: "Without the shedding of blood, there is no forgiveness."[20]

Universally, ancient cultures around the world practiced various types of sacrifices in order to appease their gods and assuage their personal sense of vulnerability to the elements and unexplainable things that were beyond their control. The Bible teaches that the original sin of man caused a breach in the created order and resulted in a chasm of separation between the Creator and the apex of his creation, humankind. God carried out the first sacrifice and offered skins to cover the shame of Adam and Eve over the sudden awareness of their nakedness before God, after they had broken His commandment not to eat of the forbidden fruit. Instead of being satisfied with all of the trees of the garden, and their fruit, which God had allowed them, they went to eat from the one tree that God said would cause them, and their offspring, great pain and suffering. As a preacher once said: "The problem was not with the apple in the tree; but rather with the pair on the ground." A great example of foreshadowing --the shedding of the blood of that first sacrifice, planned by God Himself, was a type of atonement for their sin and a covering for their guilt and shame. Thousands of years later the shedding of Jesus' blood, also planned by God Himself, made possible the forgiveness of sin for all who repent and receive God's grace offered through His son Jesus Christ.

This atonement for sin was foretold by the prophet Isaiah, writing to the Jewish people centuries before Christ would come. Isaiah said that God would send a suffering servant who would, "take up our pain and bear our suffering; being pierced for our transgressions and crushed for our iniquities; the punishment that brought us peace was on him, and by his wounds we are healed."[21] The apostle Paul, a Jewish Pharisee who later came to faith in Christ, said, "When the set time had fully come, God sent His Son, born of a woman, born under the law, that we might receive adoption to sonship and receive His Spirit into our hearts."[22] All of this took place because: "God was reconciling the world to Himself in Christ, not counting our sins against us."[23]

I was particularly struck by Jesus sweating great drops of blood and that would be my text with particular attention to the part where Jesus prayed, "If it be possible Father, let this cup of suffering pass from me; nevertheless, not my will but Thy will be done." I decided to preach on knowing God's will and using the text of Jesus's sweating great drops of blood in the Garden of Gethsemane on the night he was betrayed by one of the twelve disciples, Judas Iscariot. I spent much time reading, praying, and I believe that I nearly sweat great drops of blood myself in the process. I'm surprised I didn't do that – sweat great drops of blood – on the night of my sermon at the youth service. I remember waiting outside of Don's office at the church before the 6pm Sunday evening service with all of the other high school seniors who were playing the part of the church staff. I made the tactical mistake of asking the "associate-pastor," Brian Bailey, if he was nervous.

I am not sure what I anticipated that Brian would say, but what he said sent chills up my spine. In fair response to my forthright question, Brian assured me that he was not nervous at all, as he had participated in a good number of debate and public speaking opportunities at the Governor's School of Science and Mathematics, or something like that. In contrast, I had never done anything of any consequence, and I still had recollections of my junior high phobia of public speaking, praying, and reading that had seemed to manifest itself on the very church campus where I was about to preach a televised sermon. And I had to follow Brian Bailey! I feel as if I may start sweating great drops of blood even now just thinking back about it.

Brian did a very fine job, as everyone expected. I remember that he quoted the prominent evangelical intellectual Josh McDowell, who was an expert on apologetics. Then he was finished, and it was my turn. I don't remember much about my actual time in the pulpit, but I must have given an invitation at the end of my sermon. An invitation is the traditional response time at the end of a sermon where those in attendance have the opportunity to walk down to the front of the auditorium to pray, speak with a minister, give evidence of their desire to unite with Christ in faith, join the church, or any other such momentous decision.

Again, I do not know what I said except that I had planned to preach on Jesus in the Garden of Gethsemane sweating great drops of blood and committing Himself to the will of God with regard to the Cross, saying: "Not my will but thy will be done." It seemed to me that I finished the whole 15-minute sermon in just two and a half minutes, and I may have. I don't recall being instructed to give an invitation and, as I said above, I am not certain that I even gave one. I do recall that a number of people came down to pray, and it seemed like a divine moment in my perception. Perhaps they were thanking God that the service was over.

I remember being particularly struck that our Staff Minister of Music, Dennis Butcher, was on his knees praying with a most earnest look and some tears streaming down his face. I had been in his junior high choir, the Young Musicians, before becoming a choir drop out. Our row of boys was cutting up at practice one Sunday afternoon, and he called us out and made us sing the part individually, presumably to discern who was ruining the melodious mix or perhaps just to regain control of the group. I did not like singing and I only participated in the choir because it was imposed upon me by the "church-system" in those days, including my parents.

When Mr. Butcher pointed a finger at each junior high boy, it was his turn to sing the part solo. When he pointed at me for my turn, I tried to sing but my pre-pubescent voice betrayed my lack of training or talent. In front of everyone, my voice cracked, and I was thoroughly embarrassed as there were probably 50 boys and girls in the choir that day. As soon as I had attempted and failed to sing well, I got up and walked out never to return to choir again. Perhaps that backstory had something to do with Mr. Butcher praying on his knees with apparent emotion at the end of our youth service that night.

So, in spite of being "the pastor" for one week at Youth Week, I had never been able to sustain any long-term consistency as a follower of Jesus Christ after my salvation. Now, here I was, a new sailor on the USS *Saratoga* with everything in the future before me and the opportunity to turn over a new leaf, as my Dad used to say. Most pointedly, I had just heard a brand-new "baby" Christian, John Picarilli, take a bold stand for Christ. Picarilli did outrank me in OI Division as he was a Third-Class Petty Officer (OS3) and I was but a mere Seaman Apprentice (OSSA) on account of getting busted down a paygrade for fighting at OS "A" School.

In my mind though, I outranked Picarilli as a Christian because I had been saved nearly three years previous at a summer youth camp in 1982. I remember thinking of myself as an "Old Christian" at the age of 18, in contrast with this guy Picarilli, a mere babe in Christ. He really needed my help; after all, I had even preached a sermon once. It is kind of funny to reflect upon it now but, truthfully, I had a fairly good handle on the basics of Christian discipleship at that point even if I had done a poor job of living them out on a daily basis. My youth ministry experience at the First Baptist Church of Charlotte and the upbringing my parents had instilled within me had contributed to a firm foundation of Christian understanding that I would soon have occasion to put into practice. Now it was time to decide what I was going to do with that knowledge. How would I choose to build upon that foundation?

CHAPTER 10

LIBERTY CALL!

John Picarilli, a brand-new baby Christian, had taken a stand for Christ in a strong, forthright, and winsome manner. The thing that struck me most about Picarilli, who had been raised as a Catholic in Philadelphia, was that he seemed unashamed to bear witness to his recent conversion experience. The truth is, that I had largely been reluctant to differentiate myself as a committed Christian from my friends in high school. The same reluctance had characterized my half-hearted efforts to live the Christian life during my first nine months in the Navy. Yet, here I was, for the first time in my memory, seeing firsthand the power and impact of a young man who was willing to share his faith publicly with his friends and colleagues, even if it cost him something.

As I lay sleeplessly in my rack that night, and I don't know how else to put it, I wrestled with the Spirit of God. The Bible recounts Jacob wrestling with God over the course of a long night after many years of wandering from God and ending in futile frustration. Jacob was the son of Isaac and the grandson of Abraham. For many years, Jacob's life did not match his spiritual heritage, and he was undistinguished by any noteworthy accomplishments. In fact, Jacob's life was marked by strife, and his relationships were characterized by deceit and loss until that "wrestling match."

With regard to the Biblical account of Jacob wrestling with God, some say that he encountered an angel that night. Other commentators refer to this as a theophany, which is a supernatural appearance of God to man. Whatever the case, the tenacious Jacob held onto the heavenly being and said, "I will not let you go until you bless me." The transcendent visitor replied, "What is your name?" The troubled offspring of Abraham and Isaac identified himself, saying, "I am Jacob!" In the Hebrew tongue Jacob meant "trickster' or "grabber," since Jacob had grabbed the heel of his first-born twin brother Esau at birth, and they had competed for the birthright of preeminence ever since.

The scripture records that Jacob's wrestling partner declared, "Your name will no longer be Jacob, but Israel, because you have struggled with God and with humans and you have overcome." After asking the heavenly being his name, but receiving no answer, Jacob was so moved by the experience that he gave the site of the encounter the place name "Peniel," which, in Hebrew, means "face of God." The significance of what happened that night led Jacob to conclude: "I saw God face to face, and yet my life was spared." The site of the wrestling match had become holy ground since Jacob saw the "face of God" there. Jacob's hip was wrenched in the all-night wrestling match, but he gained the new name, Israel, which is thought to mean "he who struggles with God." Perhaps it goes without saying, but Jacob, renamed Israel, became the namesake of an entire race of people. That this race of people, and their unique relationship with their God, would be central throughout the historical narrative of the Bible makes Jacob's experience in Genesis chapters 25-38 all the more significant.

I certainly cannot say that I saw a visible being that night on the *Saratoga*, or that I wrestled a physical presence but, in my soul, there had been a contest for my will. I remember thinking that if I really dedicated myself to the Lord and turned away from sin, my life would appear to be in stark contrast to the majority of my peers on the ship. Sailors, in those days, had a collective reputation as cussing, drinking, carousing, hell-raisers, and that was a fairly accurate portrayal. If I turned my life over to the Lord completely, it terrified me to think how different I would be from my shipmates. Until that time, I had typically retained one foot in the world with the other foot tentatively planted in my Christian identity. Consequently, as the Scripture describes, I was "blown by the wind, tossed by the sea, double-minded, and unstable" in all that I did."[24]

The insight that the Holy Spirit convicted me with that night was that I needed to commit to the LORD wholeheartedly, and not concern myself any more with what others thought of me. I was worried that if I lived for God, people would ask me what was different about me, or why did I not act as everyone else did? I was afraid to be to be different, and to explain that the difference was due to Christ in my life. In short, I was afraid to be a witness for Jesus Christ. But now, I had seen a brand-new Christian, John Picarilli, take a stand for Christ with courage and freedom from the constraints of the opinions of others. The wrestling match in my soul concluded sometime during the night and, like Jacob, I awoke the next day with a new identity. I had surrendered my will to the greater purpose of serving God and being a witness for Jesus Christ onboard my new home, the USS *Saratoga*.

In retrospect, I know now that I was truly a Christian from my conversion at Camp Cheerio back in the summer of 1982. The Holy Spirit, who affects the new birth "of the Spirit," which Jesus talked about in John chapter 3, had come into my life. The Holy Spirit, or indwelling presence of God, is essential to the Christian life so much so that the Apostle Paul said, "If anyone does not have the Spirit of Christ, they do not belong to Jesus Christ."[25] I know with certainty that I had the Holy Spirit before I came to the *Saratoga*, as a direct result of my conversion to Christ at Camp Cheerio in 1982. For the most part, prior to my wrestling match with God that night, the Holy Spirit did not have all of me. In other words, I had all of God, but God did not have all of me. God convicted me of my partial commitment through the witness of a brand-new Christian who stood up for his faith. That young man's brave act of public witness had become, for me, one of the greatest gamechangers of my entire life!

I don't recall all of the details of those early days on the *Saratoga* but, somehow, I got connected with a group of believers at the Maranatha Christian Servicemen's Center, which was not far beyond the security gate at Mayport Naval Station. Outside of military bases, it is not uncommon to find bars, strip clubs, pawn shops and various other establishments that cater to and sometimes prey upon young military service personnel. In my new chosen lifestyle, I decided to bypass those types of places which I had visited on occasion in the few weeks previous. Just as Jacob, who wrestled through the night with God and came out with a new identity, I had a new bearing and a sense of obligation to live for Christ. And just as importantly, I had a new sense of boldness that came from the indwelling Holy Spirit.

How I found the Maranatha Christian Servicemen's Center is not clear in my mind at this point. It was a residential ministry center in the Atlantic Beach area about four miles from the Naval base. Residing at Maranatha, there was a good number of brothers in Christ from various Navy ships that were homeported at Mayport Naval Station. Shortly after my arrival to the *Saratoga* in late March until the ship pulled out on its Med/IO Deployment on 26 August 1985, I lived among the dozen or so young Christian sailors that paid a modest stipend for one of the bunks at the homelike structure four miles from the base front gate. In addition to several bunkrooms, there were bathrooms, a kitchen, and a worship center for singing, teaching, praying and the like. Providentially, there was also a Popeye's Chicken within a short walk from Maranatha, and I quickly came to grips with the symbiotic relationship between Christians and chicken.

During those four or five months between the time I joined the crew of the *Saratoga* and our departure for the Med, we were often at sea in our pre-deployment work-up phase. It was always nice having a place to come home to when we pulled back into homeport from nearby excursions in the Jacksonville Operating Area, or the more distant Caribbean Sea. The man in charge of the Christian Servicemen's Center was Don Kalina. Don was probably in his early sixties, single, and he often spoke of his divine call to provide ministry to the sailors at Mayport Naval Station. His elderly mother resided at the center, but I don't remember her coming out of her room very often. The guys who lived at the center were an unusual assortment of sailors from various ships. Most notably, this Baptist boy had found himself among a group, Don Kalina included, of charismatic Christians.

If you are unfamiliar with the wide range of sub-varieties within the larger Christian community, then you would likely have found the idiosyncrasies of the folks at the Maranatha Christian Servicemen's Center as unusual as I did. Let's just say that they were enthusiastic, and a few were strange. They did seem to love the Lord, and they were not ashamed of Jesus Christ. That was our common bond. It was providential for me to have a place where I was removed from the rabble that lived on a Navy ship when in port. I say that with all due respect to the rabble.

I did not know of any other Christians in my division, or even on the *Saratoga*, at that point several months before the cruise. Strangely, I have but little recollection of John Picarilli, the human catalyst for my newfound identity, after my recommitment to Jesus Christ. He was an older sailor in his mid-twenties, and I was a newbie at the age of eighteen. That alone might have been an obstacle to the development of our friendship. As I recall, he soon cooled from his previous level of public piety and resumed business as usual with his buddies on the ship. I surely hope he has since found spiritual encouragement from others of the type that he provided to me when I needed it most.

In those early days, when in port, and not on duty, I caught the bus, or rode my bicycle out to the servicemen's center; which was about four miles from the base security gate in the direction of Atlantic Beach. That the Center, itself, was just a few blocks from the beach made it all the more interesting. The beaches close to the base were a bit sketchy in those days. Reflecting upon it, my existence in the berthing compartment of OI Division while at sea and the Maranatha Christian Servicemen's Center, when in port, was a very spartan existence. But I can tell you that I felt happy, content, and challenged in an adventurous sort of way, since I was a Navy sailor with a newly adopted mission to be a soldier for Jesus Christ.

On Sundays, Brother Don would load up the guys at the center in an old bus and we would drive to one or another of the charismatic churches in the Jacksonville area with which he shared some connection. The one I remember most was in downtown Jacksonville. On these occasions and in our worship services at the center itself, I saw tambourine shakers, Hebrew dancers, the blowing of Shofars (Ram's Horns) and all sorts of worship expressions, some of which seemed pretty odd to me. It was certainly a far cry from the worship services I had attended in my home church or the chapel services that I had frequented since arriving at boot camp. Most notably, the emphasis seemed often to be upon speaking in unknown tongues. Being raised in the First Baptist Church of Charlotte, I knew nothing about this phenomenon except that it was very important to my new Christian friends, particularly Don, and that they sincerely wanted me to receive the gift of tongues myself.

It was also curious to me how some of my Baptist friends back home seemed to get rather uptight when I corresponded with them asking questions about the subject. In fact, when I mentioned this new place of residence to my parents, along with the affinity for tongues-speaking among my new housemates, they promptly referred me to the Associate Pastor of our church for immediate intervention. I received a letter from Reverend Joe Burnette, the Associate Pastor at First Baptist Charlotte, affirming my church attendance and pursuit of Christ but also cautioning me about placing too much emphasis upon any external sign that could be imitated or that might draw my attention away from Christ Himself.

Over the course of time, while deployed on the cruise, this soft divide in the body of Christ between charismatics and non-charismatics would be a persistent reality, but we managed it well on the ship. Our Command Chaplain Hugo Hammond, the man who baptized us in the Jordan River, was ordained by the Assemblies of God, a charismatic-Pentecostal denomination. The second ranked Protestant Chaplain was Chris Xenakis, a Baptist. So, you can see that the charismatic to Baptist spectrum of believers onboard the ship went all the way to the top of the chaplaincy department.

While I had been raised as a Baptist, there were things about the charismatics that impressed me. The thing that I loved most about the charismatics was their zeal for Christ. They were typically unashamed of the Lord and willing to speak boldly as His witness. The downside, which characterized some of these charismatics, was that their spiritual zeal often went hand in hand with a loose grip upon the Bible, or at least a haphazard manner of interpreting the Scripture with a propensity for the unusual and the sensational. Don Kalina had often affirmed my knowledge of the Bible, as a Baptist, and urged the other brothers to stay in the Word. I really felt loved and appreciated at Maranatha, even though they thought I was lacking something that they sincerely wished for me to have.

I remember really struggling over this matter of who was right and who was wrong between the Baptist evangelical types or the charismatic evangelicals. The primary line of differentiation between the two groups seemed to be the position one took with regard to speaking in tongues. Later after we deployed on our Med cruise, I had a very good Christian friend on the ship, Jeffrey Borja. He was about my age and from the Philippines. Jeff was very pro-charismatic and had come to Christ through the charismatic Catholic renewal in the Philippines. After apprehending the hijackers of the *Achille Lauro* and transiting into the Indian Ocean through the Suez Canal, the *Saratoga* was rewarded with a port visit into Singapore for a long week at Christmas of 1985. A good number of the guys on the ship who were believers connected with a Christian ministry in Singapore called Harvester Baptist Mission.

I was with a handful of Christian sailors in a McDonalds in Singapore when we met some young Chinese Christians who were fluent in English. Either we overheard them, or they overheard us, talking about the Lord, and a wonderful relationship had its beginning in the McDonalds in Singapore over Big Macs. As it turned out, these young Chinese Christians were affiliated with the Harvester Baptist Mission, there in Singapore. It was an independent Baptist group from Texas that had been in Singapore for a long time and had developed a strong indigenous ministry there. They were reaching a good number of Mandarin-speaking Chinese people. When these Chinese Christians invited us back to Harvester Baptist Mission, it was the beginning of a most memorable relationship, which would include several dozen visitors from the *Saratoga* to Harvester before we pulled out to sea a week later.

The Leadership at Harvester arranged for the sailors from the Saratoga to take a tour of a Hindu Temple and to sit in on a Buddhist funeral in order to give us a taste of the religious diversity of Singapore. Clanging gongs, body paint on the priests, and fruit offerings to a multitude of statues representing various gods of the Hindu pantheon were some of the more striking recollections of the Hindu Temple, not to mention the priests drinking cow urine. The Buddhist funeral was also unforgettable and seemed to center around a dramatic display of grief for the dead and burning elaborate papier-mâché representations of worldly possessions which they hoped to transfer in some metaphysical way to accompany the deceased into the hereafter. At the Buddhist funeral we attended, a near to scale papier-mâché Mercedes Benz was lit in flames as an offering for the loved one now departed. The cremains of the deceased were placed into an urn, which would be taken out and worshipped on special occasions when ancestors were revered to advance them along into the afterlife.

All of this exposure was to give us a window into the religious life of the local people who worshipped in the traditions of their fathers and mothers, but did not have a clear plan of salvation or the assurance of eternal life based upon the merits of a sinless savior like Jesus Christ. In contrast to Christianity, other religions all tend to rely upon the merits of the person, or the goodwill offerings of their loved ones left behind to advance them in the afterlife. Christianity, on the other hand, emphasizes the unconditional love of God and the free grace and forgiveness of sins that God offers to anyone who sincerely believes and live out their faith demonstrating its authenticity. And Harvester Baptist Mission seemed to be living out their faith with great authenticity in Singapore!

It was a striking experience to see for ourselves the work of these devoted missionaries, and I can tell you that the leaders of the Harvester Baptist Mission were as sincere and earnest as any of the various missionaries we encountered in our travels. They took great pains to introduce us to the local culture and to see that we had fun while enjoying it. They even got us to try the notorious Durian fruit, which we were warned: "tastes like heaven but smells like hell." The secret to its consumption, as I recall, was to hold your nose while you eat the stuff. We had many laughs over that culinary experience and the missionaries enjoyed seeing us initiated into their adopted culture in this manner. The Chinese believers at Harvester seemed to enjoy our distaste for the heavenly, yet hellish, fruit even more than their Texas brethren, who ran the Harvester Mission. It was a good time for all!

After a full day of touring Singapore with the missionaries, we returned to the Harvester Mission for evening worship services. The tenured missionary, who was an older man from Texas, preached a very strong sermon from the Bible that night. I remember really enjoying the sermon and feeling thankful for the opportunity to worship God with the large assortment of Navy sailors, Chinese Christians, and American missionaries in attendance. What was unforgettable, however, was that when the sermon was over, Jeffrey Borja, my charismatic shipmate from the Philippines, was deeply affected by the sermon. In fact, Jeff had walked down front in the worship center at the public invitation time for prayer with the missionary after the sermon was over. I wasn't sure what he was thinking, but I was glad to see that he had apparently found this experience so meaningful.

Afterward, Jeff and I were back onboard the *Saratoga* talking about the experience at Harvester, and he told me that he got saved after hearing the sermon and responding to the invitation to receive Jesus Christ. The preacher had explained the gospel of Jesus and our need to individually repent of our sin and believe in Christ's atoning death for our sins. I was a bit shaken and asked, "weren't you already saved?" To my surprise, Jeff said that he did not think that he had been truly saved prior to that night at the Harvester Mission in Singapore. Trying to process this admission by my friend, I said: "What about your speaking in tongues, Jeff?" He shook his head and muttered that he must have done that all by himself. Jeff and I mutually concluded that he had apparently put his faith in his experience of speaking in tongues, and that as an outward sign he had relied upon the tongues as the basis and proof of his relationship with Jesus Christ. This outward expression without an internal possession had left Jeffrey Borja empty. That was our mutual conclusion as I recall.

The realization that had hit me on that liberty call from the ship in Singapore was that Christ, the Holy Spirit, the gospel, and the Word of God were the things that brought about salvation and authentic spiritual growth. Any competing emphasis upon any experience, however sincere that emphasis might be could actually result in someone being misled into emotional experientialism and a pseudo-spirituality. I'm not declaring that speaking in tongues is not a valid experience; but I will say that an inordinate emphasis upon it is disproportionate in weight to the few references in the Bible on the subject. That fact should be a caution that something is amiss if an undo emphasis is placed upon the believer speaking in tongues.

By the time the *Saratoga* was in Singapore for Christmas in 1985, the spiritual awakening movement had been growing ever since the baptism of over 100 young sailors in the Jordan River on 09 November 1985. After my experience at Harvester Baptist Mission in Singapore, it seemed that my spiritual form was really beginning to take its shape. After Jeffrey Borja's salvation experience at Harvester, I had a crystalizing moment when I realized the importance of the gospel, the Bible, and the Holy Spirit over and above outward signs which could be mimicked and a diversion from the most important things. My new identity in Christ would take from the charismatics a zeal, a strong appreciation for the Holy Spirit within us, and a boldness in my witness for Jesus Christ. From my home church, particularly the influence of Charles Page and Don Brock, along with the habit of reading and critical thinking I had gained from my upbringing, came a natural inclination toward the authority of the Scriptures. That inclination reflected my Baptist heritage, since the authority of Scripture alone is the basis for all other Baptist beliefs. I was beginning to find my path forward in God's kingdom.

Maranatha Christian Servicemen's Center had been a providential blessing in my life at a time when I probably needed such a place and a people to help me in those early steps after arriving to join the crew of the *Saratoga*. My time at the Servicemen's Center, before we left for our Med/IO deployment, had definitely been a game changer for me. Yet, I felt that it was now time for me to move on as the Lord led, and He seemed to be leading me by way of Scripture and experience. I had been a faithful tither to the Maranatha Christian Servicemen's Center; giving one-tenth of my Navy salary as an E-3 (Operations Specialist Seaman) from my first days through Maranatha's door back in March, and I had continued to tithe my salary there throughout the deployment. I have no idea how many of the other guys at Maranatha tithed their navy salaries, but I had a feeling that my decision to move on from Maranatha would affect Don Kalina, both emotionally and financially.

I felt that it was important for me to write a letter to Don in order to explain myself and lessen the angst within my soul. Because of the long distance and reliance upon military flights, I knew that it would be several weeks before my letter made it back to Jacksonville Beach. In the letter, I told Don about my charismatic friend Jeffrey Borja who had found Christ through the preaching of the gospel apart from any emphasis upon the outward sign of speaking in tongues; which Jeff had previously based his salvation upon. Furthermore, I told Don that I appreciated him very much and that God had used Maranatha Christian Servicemen's Center to make a big difference in my life. The hardest part was that I told him that I would be moving in a different direction with regard to my living arrangements and my church participation upon our return to Mayport from the deployment. Since I had no other church at the moment to direct my tithe, I assured Don that I would continue to tithe to Maranatha until I returned from the cruise and united with another church.

Several weeks later, I received a reply from Don, and he told me that he would be there to meet me at the pier with some of the brothers from Maranatha when the *Saratoga* pulled back into port in a few months. Other than that, I cannot remember what his letter said, but I am pretty sure it was kind and supportive with perhaps a bit of dissuasion against my announcement to find another place of worship upon my return. Since none of my *Saratoga* shipmates had attended church, or lived in residence, at the Servicemen's Center, I had no interactions with anyone from that place during the eighth months of our deployment. I recall that before our departure on the cruise, I had not yet found any Christian fellowship onboard the Saratoga and would not until after we got underway on our deployment. God had graciously provided Maranatha as a means of encouragement and Christian discipleship during my first few months on the *Saratoga* while we were doing work ups out of Mayport Naval Station prior to our deployment.

During the first several months on our cruise, much had happened in my life and on our ship. The spiritual awakening that had taken place on the *Saratoga* during our 8-month deployment had brought a lot of people into our growing Christian fellowship group on the *Saratoga*. In my division alone, there were probably ten percent of the 70 Operations Specialists who became strongly identified with the Christian movement. An additional ten percent, or so, of OI Division was nominally, but publicly, connected to the Christian movement, and many of these developments had taken place within the eight-month time frame. I should add that these numbers are only estimates, and that they are dependent upon my best awareness and recollection.

Between our departure on August 28, 1985 and the baptism of over one hundred sailors in the Jordan River on November 12, 1985, the movement had firmly taken root. After the baptismal service on November 12th, until our return on April 16, 1986, the *Saratoga's* Christian population had increased and was growing with help from the programmatic infrastructure provided by the Chaplain's office. This infrastructure ranged from providing Sunday services in the Chapel to offering Christian-themed movies on Friday nights that were produced by Billy Graham's Worldwide Pictures. The Chaplain's Office also offered several different video seminars provided by James Dobson's Focus on the Family Ministry. All of these various programs were offered while we were at sea during the deployment. Through these opportunities for fellowship and spiritual growth, the Christian community had something to look forward to and also something to invite others to experience as well.

Recently, I had the opportunity to talk with Chaplain Hammond by telephone and he reminisced that, "We had revival on the *Saratoga*!" The Command Chaplain also commented that the movement was largely lay led; meaning that it was largely carried out by non-professional religious leadership. It was the men of the ship, itself, and mostly young men who were instrumental in living out their faith and sharing it with others. I personally benefitted from the leadership of an older petty officer, relative to me as a nineteen-year old, who organized and led small-group discipleship courses. This particularly petty officer was trained in the use of the Navigator's 2:7 Series, which emphasized Bible study and Scripture memory as a means to spiritual growth, as described in Colossians 2:7.

The Navigators are a Christian para-church ministry group that had actually begun in the Navy prior to World War II. The story of Dawson Trotman, founder of the Navigators, recounts how he began to teach Christian discipleship principles and offer Bible study to a group of young sailors from the USS *West Virginia*, which was undergoing refitting at the Long Beach Naval Shipyard in the Los Angeles area prior to World War 2. After being refitted, the USS *West Virginia*, containing a significant number of Christian sailors discipled through the Navigators program, was in Pearl Harbor on December 7, 1941, where the ship was struck by seven torpedoes and two bombs in the deadly Japanese surprise attack that would be a call to arms for the U.S. in WW2. Beyond the galvanizing effect that the Japanese attack had in initiating the American war effort, many of Dawson Trotman's navigators survived the attack, and were distributed to various other Navy ships that were being deployed during the early days of WW2. The tragic occurrence at Pearl Harbor on December 7, 1941 had the effect of spreading the ministry of the Navigators throughout the Pacific Fleet, and the movement grew in the wake of this tragedy.[26]

It is remarkable to think that some forty-five years later, the ministry of Dawson Trotman would have its impact upon me during my naval service! The greatest impact for me, personally, was in regard to Scripture memorization. The Bible teaches that the Scriptures are "breathed by God" and useful for teaching, training, and guiding the believer in God's righteousness."[27] The Navigators 2:7 discipleship book that the small groups used contained Scripture memory cards, as memorization of key Bible verses is a central part of the Navigator's approach to Christian growth and discipleship. The Scripture memorization that I had begun as a child in Bible Drill programs at the First Baptist Church of Charlotte had laid a foundation for the importance of Scripture memorization that my time on the Saratoga had intensified and built upon.

As the broadening Christian movement progressed during our deployment, we had a large number of Christian sailors who made it a point to meet up as a group, or in various small groups, to go on liberty together during our port visits. Like other groups of Saratoga sailors on liberty, we wanted to see the sights, eat the food, and soak in the international experiences made possible on a navy ship underway. Perhaps the most striking difference in our Christian group from many of the other groups of sailors, however, was our general abstinence from alcohol and avoidance of places known for sexual promiscuity like clubs, brothels, and strip joints. While a number of our shipmates were prone to head for bars and clubs, we tended to look for missionaries and Christian servicemen's centers. On several occasions we met missionaries who welcomed and hosted us in their homes and their ministry centers. Those visits were times of great fellowship and we enjoyed hanging out with Christian civilians from, or serving in, other nations.

I recall that we had a Senior Chief Petty Officer from one of the air wings who played the guitar well, and we would sing Christian choruses at the end of the night while waiting for the liberty boats which shuttled people back to the Saratoga after a long day of liberty call. Another Senior Chief Petty Officer from one of the squadrons even went with me to the NATO Base in Naples, Italy in order to help me find a pair of casual shoes, which I was in need of purchasing for use during port visits. This particular Christian senior chief was an older black man and very fatherly toward us younger Christians. I was struck that the Christian fellowship extended throughout the ranks of the enlisted sailors because it had not been that long ago that I had been doing push-ups and suffering mental anguish on a regular basis at the hands of drill instructors who were usually Chiefs (E-7s) or First Class Petty officers (E-6s).

In fact, the black senior chief who went with me to the NATO base in Naples, Italy in search of shoes must have been twenty years, or more, my senior. That particular senior chief, and the guitar playing white senior chief, were among the kindest and gentlest Christians I had ever met. Keep in mind that I probably expected them to get in my face, cuss me out, and make me do push-ups at a moment's notice. Boot camp has a way of messing with your head like that. Those fine Christian sailors of the upper echelon were a striking contrast to what we had been so recently accustomed to in our training before coming to the fleet. The spiritual awakening seemed to erase lines of rank and race among the enlisted sailors as only the gospel of Jesus Christ can do. In our fellowship onboard the *Saratoga*, there were men of various races mostly White, Black, Hispanic, and Asian. There was great respect and support for one another. The military, itself, has a way of bringing down superficial distinctions that are counterproductive to the fulfillment of its mission. The Christian gospel does so even more. That part was great!

As mentioned before, the old naval sea-going tradition required non-fraternization between officers and enlisted crewmembers. Though I cannot say with certainty that the spiritual awakening movement affected the ranks of the officers in the same manner that it did a significant number of the enlisted men, the general order of the ship and its morale was good from top to bottom. That there were cordial, respectful, and professional relations between the enlisted men and the officers of the *Saratoga*, no one can deny. As stated previously, much of the general well-being and success of the *Saratoga* during this time should be attributed to its Commanding Officer, Captain Jerry L. Unruh.

Aside from our Chaplains, no commissioned officers participated in our Bible studies or times of Christian fellowship while on liberty. I suspect that the Officers had their own Bible studies, but I do not remember hearing about them. The Officers had their own berthing areas (state rooms), dining areas (ward rooms), and liberty boat launches to be transported back and forth to the *Saratoga* at anchor when we were in port.

On several occasions, we seized the opportunity to sing Christian choruses with guitar accompaniment to the large number of drunk and disillusioned young enlisted sailors waiting in queue for the liberty boats to return them from liberty call back to the ship. At the end of night, awaiting the liberty boats which would take us back to the Saratoga after a long day in port, we enjoyed our sobriety and our Christian contentment and joy was not diminished. We felt that, in contrast to the many drunk and disorderly shipmates returning from liberty, we had spent our time well. I remember feeling compassion for those who were so drunk that they could barely walk up the gangplank to make it back to their racks. Our sincere desire to pass along the freedom we had in Christ was visible and evident to those who were interested. Over the course of that cruise, many more would be interested! The movement was growing...

CHAPTER 11
READY ROOM

On a deployed aircraft carrier, as you would expect, the squadrons, the aircraft, and the pilots are a central focus and the lifeblood of the carrier. The Ship's Company, those who are permanently attached to the ship, can number up to 3,500. That number is increased by another 1,500 personnel who make up the carrier air wing. An air wing is composed of a dozen, or so, squadrons of fixed-wing and rotary aircraft. On the *Saratoga*, the air wing included fighter squadrons (F-14s) which engage in aerial combat, attack squadrons (A-6s & A-7s) that put munitions on targets below, and various other squadrons. Saratoga's aircraft provided the Battle Group with abilities such as anti-submarine warfare, to electronic (radar jamming) warfare, aerial refueling and airborne early warning (basically a large flying radar dish attached to an airplane).

Each one of the squadrons had a ready room with their squadron designation and mascot painted in vibrant colors on the walls inside the Ready Room and on the steel doorway outside. I often passed by the ready rooms belonging to the fighter squadrons, which were the VF-103 Sluggers and the VF-74 Be-Devilers. I remember passing by others as well, but the fighter squadrons stand out in my memory because of the relative preeminence given to fighter aircraft onboard a carrier. Like everything else on a carrier, each job, or squadron, is essential to the mission of the Navy, but some just have little more panache, and so it seemed to be with the fighter squadrons.

These ready rooms contained nice captain's style chairs in rows similar to a movie theater and, there, the pilots would gather for briefings to prepare for their missions. On a carrier, the ready room has a feel as if it were the Holy of Holies, the inner sanctum where only a few may dare to go. I loved to look inside when the pilots were not there. For *Saratoga*, if and when it came down to it, the preparation for engagement with hostile forces would take place in these very rooms.

With nearly 1/3 of the ship's personnel of 5,000 men being attached to the Carrier Air Wing, an aircraft carrier is noticeably different in its composition, mission, and with regard to its crew than any other type of ship in the fleet. Everything about an aircraft carrier including its appearance, trappings, and distinctive design bears the influence of age-old naval sea-going traditions even though its modern mission takes place in the skies above.

When underway, the power and effect of the surrounding sea and air, which are the theaters of operation for an aircraft carrier, are always just a short walk from your workspace or your berthing compartment. It was always a pleasure to stand on the fantail or on one of the ship's exposed weather decks to gaze at the sea and the sky above. How anyone can look at such a vast expanse of sea and sky far removed from any light pollution at night, and with a fifty-mile line-of-sight from the upper decks during a clear day, and not have a religious experience, of sorts, completely escapes me.

OI division, to which I was attached, had been strongly affected by the spiritual awakening with anywhere from ten to twenty percent of the 70 men publicly identifying as Christian, and involved in the ministries onboard the ship including the weekly chapel services. Apparently, many others could withstand nature's revelatory aspects and were seemingly impervious to the effects of the spiritual awakening taking place onboard the *Saratoga*. Though the number of Christians grew over the months to include well over one hundred who were publicly active in the movement, there were still many others who showed no interest and, some, who even evidenced hostility. Others in OI Division may not have identified publicly with the Christian movement, but they were sympathetic and supportive. One of those was our leading Petty Officer OS1 Johnson.

As previously noted, when I initially arrived to the *Saratoga*, my Enlisted Service Record was marred with a Captain's Mast proceeding in consequence of fighting while in my previous duty station -- Operations Specialist "A" school at Dam Neck, Virginia. I am fairly certain that the upper echelon of OI Division, which included several officers, two senior chiefs, and our Leading Petty Officer Alvin Johnson, were keeping a close eye on this new addition to the division, only eighteen years old, fresh out of OS "A" School and already busted for fighting.

My experience of recommitting my life to Christ happened within several weeks after my arrival to the ship, and I had behaved myself pretty well on the *Saratoga* even before that dynamic spiritual occurrence. From the start, I was a hard worker and it wasn't long at all before my new identity as a follower of Christ began to be noticed as well.

Somewhere along the way during our deployment, I been labeled by some of my shipmates in OI Division with the comical, but perhaps a bit respectful, nickname "Father Ferrell." You may be aware that Catholic priests are routinely referred to as Father so-in-so (last name), or just plain "Father." I started taking that as a compliment when a fellow OS in my division named Blake, who was from Oakland, CA, told a group of guys in our Division at a beach party that he got nervous when I came down to the beach and joined him in bodysurfing that day because he was worried that "Father Ferrell" might try to baptize him or something. I thought that was pretty funny, and I still remember the grin on Blake's face when he relayed the story to my shipmates in my presence. Most of the ribbing like that was good natured. I actually liked the fact that our Leading Petty Officer (LPO), OS1 Alvin Johnson, had coined his own nickname for me.

With his deep scratchy chain smoker's voice and a soulish Southern drawl, OS1 made the three-letter nickname string out sounding like four or five syllables when he called me "Revvvvvvvv!" Johnson was a forty-something year old black man from Charleston, South Carolina, easily the most respected OS in our division with well over twenty years of military service that including a stint in the United States Marine Corps. Word was that OS1 had gotten busted out of the Marines for fighting, but later gained readmittance into the Navy where he received orders to Operations Specialist "A" school.

With bloodshot eyes and a cigarette nearly always hanging out of his mouth the word "Rev" seemed, somehow, rather holy coming from OS1. I guess that's debatable. Nevertheless, just to be acknowledged by my LPO, who was above any reproach in his work as a track supervisor on the Air Side of Combat Information Center, made me proud. Not to mention, as the Leading Petty Officer of our division, it fell to the LPO to write the performance evaluations on the enlisted men below him, which had considerable bearing upon their future promotions and privileges. The dude had power and he wielded it with a steady and non-pretentious hand.

Thankfully, it seemed that OS1 had taken a "liking" to me early on. Maybe it was our common experience of being busted for fighting early in our careers. Perhaps it was just the favor of God upon my life, but OS1 had nearly as big a role as Picarilli did, in terms of turning me around. Under the previous commands of Boot Camp and "A" School, my evaluations were without any extraordinary distinction.

Remember that we were advised to stay unnoticed and below the radar. Apart from the fight, I had apparently been successful in accomplishing that objective. Things changed as soon as I committed my life to Christ. I realized I had a Scriptural obligation to "do my best as unto the Lord" and present a Christian witness to my shipmates at all times.

My old work ethic manifested itself, and the decks I swabbed were as good, or better, as any of those done by others. Since the tactical responsibilities of Operations Specialists are performed in CIC and on the Bridge while at sea, there wasn't much to do in port except to be sent for more training or to apply "elbow grease" in the cleaning of our Divisional Berthing Compartment, CIC, and the surrounding passageways. It was our constant responsibility to keep these spaces immaculately clean and painted. As a new guy, you can guess that I had my fair share of such opportunities, especially when we were in port. I worked hard, as I was consciously representing the Lord before the scrutiny of the larger part of my division who were curious to see if I would walk-the-walk, as well as talk-the-talk. I worked hard and OS1 Johnson rewarded me for it.

My first set of evals from OS1 were nearly straight 4.0! We were evaluated on all sorts of things ranging from military bearing to demonstrating an understanding of CIC doctrine. I had never done anything really significant on 4.0 level...so this was a game changer for me personally. I don't know if I deserved the superlative evaluations that OS1 bestowed upon me, but they certainly contributed to me beginning to see myself in a different light. I was especially honored when OS1 invited me on liberty in Rota, Spain, which was our last stop on our Med/IO Cruise before returning back to our homeport of Mayport, Florida. I enjoyed eating paella and drinking cokes with OS1 in a restaurant in Rota and we talked about many things, including a relationship with God. I don't recall the specifics of the conversation, but I remember feeling that I was with a kindred soul and a true friend, even though there was a considerable between us.

Not everyone in the division, however, shared OS1's respect for me and my Christian convictions. I remember two persons in particular who evidenced considerable contempt for me and my beliefs. Both I will leave nameless, but they both outranked me, and one shared the same rank as OS1. From that individual, I would receive my first threat as a result of my faith, but it would not be my last. This particular threat was a threat unto death. I was threatened with the fate of being thrown overboard during the night. On a Navy ship, the Man Overboard Drills are a regular occurrence, and they are taken very seriously.

On a carrier, for example, a fall from the flight deck alone is a 70-foot plunge down to the waterline. Such a fall can be fatal in itself. Beyond the fall, the next threat is being blended into a "Bloody Mary" by the enormous propellers at the back of the ship under the water line. For example, the four propellers (known in the Navy as "screws") pushing the USS *Gerald Ford* (CVN-78), a contemporary super carrier not much larger than the *Saratoga*, are 30-tons each with a diameter of 21 feet. Beyond the four massive turning screws there are, of course, sharks that tend to follow an aircraft carrier with its generous and frequent disposal of delicious garbage from the Mess Decks and other places. But the worst thing would simply be the fate of being lost in the vast expanse of sea with a jolly good carrier steaming off and over the horizon.

When an upper-level Petty Officer told me that he and some others were going to throw me overboard, and he did not appear to be joking, I was in a mild state of disbelief. But I was not afraid. I knew that the Bible told a story where a crowd of people were interrogating Jesus, and they did not like his answers. In fact, they took up stones to finish him off. The story recounts how Jesus walked away from among them because it was not His time.[28]

I had the confidence that the LORD would watch over me, and besides that I had done nothing wrong. I had simply gone into the TV lounge of OI Division to use the ship's phone line to call a friend in another division at the other end of the ship to arrange plans for liberty once we pulled into port the next day. When I went into the lounge that was adjacent to our OI Division Berthing Space, the room was packed with about a dozen OS's who were watching pornographic video tapes. As soon as I opened the door of the TV room in order to walk in to use the phone, the content of their viewing was quickly evident, and I turned around to walk out.

It is not that I was any different, physiologically speaking, from my shipmates in the TV Room, or that I lacked interest in anything related to attractive young women. In fact, at the Thanksgiving holiday, we actually had some very special guests to come on board and join us for our entertainment while we were steaming out in the Indian Ocean. Can you believe it was the Dallas Cowboy Cheerleaders?! Don't let anybody tell you the Marine Corps is better! These were some fine-looking ladies and lucky for us in CIC, we had air conditioning. It was very hot everywhere else at that time of the year where we were sailing. That's probably why the Dallas Cowboy Cheerleaders chose to hang out with the OS's in Combat Information Center, and we were all happy to oblige! And call it luck, or maybe providence, but I actually got to spend the better part of my first two-hour watch rotation hanging out with two of the cheerleaders that day!

I was keeping up the large surface plot board for the benefit of the TAO (Tactical Action Officer), who sat in his VIP Chair less than ten yards in front of me. It was the odd responsibility of OS's to know how to write backwards, yes backwards, so we could plot contacts on the other side of the board. Writing the letters and numbers enabled the TAO to view the surface plot unobstructed from his side of the large clear plexiglass board. I was on the two hour-watch station sitting on a long bench behind the surface plot board. This bench provided the only open seating in CIC. Nearly every other seat was occupied by the OSs standing watch overseeing the various surveillance consoles and radar screens.

You may not believe me, but I had two gorgeous Dallas Cowboy Cheerleaders sitting with me on the bench behind the surface plot boards during most of my two-hour watch. I'm sure I've never grinned so much in two hours, nor did I ever enjoy serving my country as much as I did that day. The contingent of celebrity cheerleaders had remained on the ship for two nights before launching from the flight deck on a large COD to return to the States. I'm sure everyone hated to see them go and maybe even a few tears were shed upon their departure. Oddly enough, the guys in the laundry division reportedly cut up the bedsheets upon which the cheerleaders had slept and turned them into marketable souvenir strips of linen with a perfumed scent. I thought it was a waste of money and, besides that, I didn't really trust the guys in laundry. All I can say is, "God bless Texas!"

But back in the TV lounge, I knew that my witness for Christ was on the line. I knew that if I remained there, as the porn video was being shown, even if just for a few minutes to make a phone call, my witness would be compromised. Plus, I might not want to leave if I stayed even for a minute. Such is the power of the sex drive that the Creator gave us to ensure the procreation of our species, which was intentionally created in His image. In addition, the Bible reveals that our sexual dimension is in keeping with God's intent to endow us with pleasure and intimacy in marriage, the institution that God purposefully designed to safeguard the lifelong commitment between a man and a woman.[29]

Yet, why is it that, with regard to sex, we see such frequent examples of a good thing gone bad. There were plenty of bad examples on a Navy ship, particularly when the sailors were turned loose after weeks at sea with a short window for acting out in the various foreign ports into which we pulled into for some adventure and excitement. The power of sexuality was evident in the constant barrage of exploitative commercial advertising on signs in every seaport town. Europe is especially decadent with regard to fleshly advertising. There were prostitutes plying their trade visibly on street corners, in drinking establishments, and in entertainment venues that were discussed shamelessly by some of their patrons who called the *Saratoga* home. The same goes for the civilian world too today when sex trafficking and the sexual abuse of children continues to make headlines.

I had but a split second to decide what I would do at that moment in the TV lounge. Well, I did exactly what Joseph, the Hebrew slave sold into Potiphar's House, did when he was grabbed by his master's wife for illicit purposes; I ran.[30] Well, actually I walked. I walked straight to the nearby OI Division office to use the phone there so that I could arrange my liberty plans with a friend during our upcoming port visit. By the way, I did observe a noticeable trend that porn viewing in the TV Lounge seemed to have a sharp uptick just before port visits. I guess it had something to do with the nickname sailors gave to porn in those days, which was the rather innocuous term "Training Films." I suppose my shipmates were brushing up on their training for the upcoming port visit. The Navy did seem to emphasize training for just about everything. At any rate, I stuck my head into the divisional office, where sat at least one of our Senior Chiefs, OS1 Johnson, another OS of similar rank, and one or two others that I can not recall.

I asked that group of higher ups: "May I use the phone for a quick call to a squadron berthing compartment?" Keep in mind that the ship was over three football fields long and with multiple levels reached by ladders and stairways, and the stairways, which we called ladders, looked like ladders themselves. To get from one end of the ship to another was really a long hike. In response to my respectful request to use the office phone, one of the higher ups in the office replied: "Ferrell, use the damn phone in the TV Lounge!" I said: "Well...I can't go in the TV lounge right now Senior Chief." "Well...Why the hell not," someone replied. "They're watching Training Films," I said.

Upon that revelation, everyone in the office looked up from their paperwork and did a double take on me. Well, that had apparently gotten their attention! Then, I was politely given the privilege to come in to use the phone in the Division Office to make my call. I went on liberty and had a great time and thought nothing more about it. Certainly, the higher-ups knew what was being watched in the TV room because the sound effects of the "Training Films" could sometimes be heard in the nearby passageways. So, I didn't see any big deal at all about giving an honest answer to the question: "Why can't you go into the TV Lounge?"

A few days passed, and I had forgotten about the phone call, the TV lounge, and the whole episode. But someone else who had been in the office that day had apparently not forgotten. When we were back at sea after the port visit, one of the upper level OS Petty Officers who had been present in the Divisional Office that day confronted me. That particular petty officer was at least ten years older than me and he outranked me by three very significant paygrades. It is my faint recollection that we were up in the forecastle space, where the anchor chain is kept, on the occasion that he confronted me. It was an out of the way compartment in the ship without much foot traffic. I believe that the space was sometimes used for jumping rope and calisthenics, and that was my purpose in being there, but I can't recall specifically.

The offended man appeared belligerent as he recounted the incident involving the TV lounge. He accused me of going into the Division Office just to rat out my shipmates for watching "Training Films." He said that he, and some others, would soon throw me overboard. I just walked away, like Jesus did, and nothing ever happened. I actually had no more trouble from that individual ever again so far as I recall. I can still see his menacing face and I distinctly remember his name. In fact, now that I am a pastor, I think I'm going to tell the Lord about him.

When people with different value systems and differing points of view live in such proximity to one another for extended periods of time, conflicts are inevitable. But, as I mentioned before, conflict was not a common occurrence on the *Saratoga*, and I never witnessed an actual fight among the crew, not once. Race relations were amazingly good, and the integration of so many people from different backgrounds, races, cultures, and religions with the achievement of equanimity still amazes me to this day. The driving factors of our unity undoubtedly were a Commander in Chief, namely Ronald Reagan, who had established a clear course as to our mission in the armed services, as well as a Commanding Officer on the Saratoga, Jerry Unruh, who was in missional alignment with the priorities of the President. This unity in the chain of command gave way to an unrelenting pursuit of the purpose to make America the best it could be and defeat Soviet communism in the process. Such adherence to a clear missional purpose had an effect of superseding petty differences and superfluous characteristics. Nothing mattered but doing the job.

Even among the visible Christian fellowship group onboard the *Saratoga*, which easily included over a hundred enlisted sailors who were pretty close, I recall one particular season of conflict that caused a noticeable degree of division among us. The situation to which I refer was the upcoming and planned crossing of the equator in the Indian Ocean. As mentioned before, centuries of naval tradition have maintained that sailors who cross the equator and are initiated become trusty shellbacks. The practice of line crossing ceremonies at sea goes back at least to the Phoenicians, who did all sorts of things to appease the gods, including human sacrifice, to ensure lucrative maritime trade and safe passage back home. The Vikings were another notable culture that practiced such superstitions to ensure safe oceanic travels.

The shell-back initiation tradition actually claims to honor the ancient Roman god Neptune, who was thought to be, in olden days, the god of the sea. Neptune corresponded to the even more ancient Greek-god of the sea known as "Poseidon." In those ancient days, mariners initiated as shellbacks after crossing the equator were thought to become, on some level, sons and daughters of the Roman god Neptune. The pagan religious backgrounds of the shellback initiations caused some of the Christians onboard the *Saratoga* to have understandable misgivings in regard to the origins of the line-crossing ceremony.

In fact, the Christian community onboard the *Saratoga* was split right down the middle on the issue of participation in the line-crossing ceremony. True to the good leadership of the *Saratoga*, and the value placed upon freedom of conscience in keeping with our national heritage, we were told that conscientious objectors could sit out the line crossing ceremony, if they chose to do so. Those who were against participating in the initiation argued that it was pagan, and even devilish. Those Christians in our fellowship who were determined to participate in the initiation felt that since these gods were not real, participation was a moot point and no harm was done. In keeping with the reasoning of the Apostle Paul in his correspondence to the Corinthian Church regarding their concern over eating meat offered to idols, Christians who chose to participate in the initiation felt that they had Christian liberty to do so.[31] Those who chose to participate believed it was just good clean fun, even if it resembled torture.

Many conversations took place on the Mess Decks in the weeks leading to the day of crossing and, in the end, everybody pretty much followed their conscience and gave space for differing perspectives. For me, it seemed right to participate, get the award, and show the broader company of sailors that Christians were not sissies. The degree to which the initiation had been hyped with various accounts from experienced shellbacks about the horrible things they would do to us pollywogs, probably caused everyone not yet initiated to pause and consider the path of conscientious objection.

The worst torture was having to swim under water in a long and deep container, maybe ten yards long, that had been filled half-full of a green colored liquid containing all sorts of garbage and vomit, along with other unnamed fluids and solids. If you surfaced before reaching the end, you were beaten upon the head with short sections of firehose. We were lined up and required to eat a cherry from a seated fat man's belly button, and many other calculated abuses were heaped upon us all in the name of fun and games. All of this was done on the flight deck, and it had the appearance and feel of a cross between a raucous and well attended carnival and the Texas Chainsaw Massacre. But in the end, it was a relief to be through with it, and I proudly received my Shellback Certificate. I almost regret that I did not stay in the Navy long enough to turn the tables and initiate some folks myself.

It seems worthwhile to mention at this point that Captain Unruh was very visible and even participated in the initiations. As a Fighter Pilot in Viet Nam, the Captain had long been a Shellback and he seemed quite at home superintending over the whole affair. One of the pictures in our Cruise Book shows the Captain, with a mischievous grin on his face, standing over our Ship's Navigator, surprisingly a pollywog, while the Navigator is bent over and appears to be vomiting. In deference to both, I complied with the Admiral's request to leave that photo out of this narrative, and I only relay this story to demonstrate his humanity and collegial involvement with the crew. That these two men are close friends to this day is a testament to the bonds of brotherhood among great men who serve together. If you can get your hands on the Cruise Book, you can see the picture yourself!

During all of those days at sea on deployment, I had the growing sense that I was being prepared for something else. Looking back on it, I have no doubt that what took place upon the *Saratoga* was a spiritual awakening. Such religious and cultural movements happen when the Spirit of God moves in such a way as to affect a significant number of conversions which result in a positive Christ-centered change in the spiritual and moral climate of a larger group of people.[32]

All that we experienced onboard the *Saratoga*, particularly during its 1985-86 deployment, was used of God to shape my life, faith, and character. A widely-loved Scripture passage in Romans 8:28 says: "And we know that God causes all things to work together for good to those who love Him and are called according to His purpose." There were many, like me, who felt that something very special had taken place on the *Saratoga* and that God would use these experiences to bring about even greater things in the future. What so many had experienced on our deployment was, like the Ready Room, a place for gathering and preparation for the mission, and the battles, that lay ahead.

CHAPTER 12

FLIGHT OPS

One of the thrills of life at sea on an aircraft carrier was watching flight operations. Unless you worked on the flight deck, which is considered to be one of the most dangerous job sites in the world, or on the bridge, a rather safe space in comparison, you would not likely have an authorized vantage point from which to watch the show. Night flight operations were especially mesmerizing as the afterburners of the jets emitted a dragon's breath of fire, and the accompanying noise of jet engines lets you know that you are in the presence of lethal power. The present technology on in-service carriers can catapult a 45,000-pound airplane up into the sky from 0-165 mph in two seconds. That is likely a bit faster than the four steam catapults on the *Saratoga* were capable of launching, but the slim margin of difference would hardly be noticeable.

Those who worked on the bridge included the captain, the navigator, the officer of the deck (OOD), a few quartermasters who worked with navigational charts, and two boatswain's mates. The latter two were the helmsman who manned the wheel to direct *Saratoga*'s course and, the lee-helmsman who controlled the speed of the ship by communicating with the engine room personnel below. Both, of course, were commanded by the Captain or the OOD.

In addition to these vital positions on the captain's bridge, one Operations Specialist was always present to maintain a surface plot board. This OS received the necessary information for the board from the surface radar operator below in CIC via our sound-powered phone system.

The surface radar operator called out bearings and ranges to all of the surface contacts through the sound-powered headphone set. The two OSs maintaining surface plot boards in CIC and on the Bridge could update their boards with the bearings and ranges of all surface vessels within a prescribed range relative to the *Saratoga*'s ever-changing position. In addition, we had to calculate the course and speed of every vessel in our area of operation. We had an amazing machine called the Dead Reckoning Tracer (DRT) that looked like an architect's drawing table. The DRT kept our Latitude & Longitude position displayed by means of a compass within the DRT tabletop that moved in sync relative to the ships position, course, and speed. Butcher paper was laid over the glass tabletop of the DRT and the lighted compass within the glass case moved in accordance with the ship's movement. The DRT operator would plot the positions of all other ships in our area on the butcher paper from the bearings and ranges called out by the radar operator. By drawing a straight line on the butcher paper through at least three previous fixed points of any vessel, you could calculate its course and speed and project it's anticipated course. Let's just say that we probably used more butcher paper than most butcher's do in keeping up with the ever-changing position of the Saratoga and the vessels that were in our area of movement. But we always had a visible record of the ship's exact position as well as all of the vessels in our area. The safe navigation of the ship was vital to our mission and crucial to successful flight operations. All of this pertinent navigational information had to be available to the Captain and to the Tactical Action Officer at a glance so they could make decisions very quickly, and as they thought best.

When flight operations were going on the personnel on the Bridge had to exercise great discipline to complete their vital assignments while we tried to sneak as much viewing of flight operations as was safely possible. There was no better seat in the house to watch flight ops than from the captain's bridge, which was just a few stories above the flight deck and looked directly down upon the action. Since most sailors on the carrier did not have a front row seat for flight ops and yet every position on the ship is vital to its successful operation, Captain Unruh authorized occasional air shows with" fly-bys" and live ordinance drops on practice targets. Once the planes were launched into the air from the catapults, the Captain gave the all clear over the ship's 1-MC announcing system, and all whose obligations could be suspended until later to watch the show.

Especially exciting, on these *Saratoga* airshow occasions, was the much-anticipated breaking of the sound barrier by at least one of the jets performing above the carrier. When a jet travels faster than the speed of sound, a sonic boom is heard on the ground below just after the airplane passes overhead. This delayed sonic boom occurs in response to a change in pressure as the jet outruns all of the air pressure and sound waves moving ahead of it. Once the speeding airplane has passed over the flight deck, the pressure disturbance waves radiate toward the ground causing the sonic boom.[33] It was always a crowd pleaser! If we didn't get at least one sonic boom, unhappy crew members might have wanted a refund. No airshow was complete without the "Boom!" The actual speed of sound is variable depending upon the altitude and air temperature but Mach 1, or the speed of sound, is around 761 miles per hour at sea level on a temperate day, and that is pretty fast.

No *Saratoga* air show would be complete without the Gunner's Mates unleashing the Phalanx Close-in Weapons System, or Sea-Wiz. This ship borne defense gunnery is basically a high-tech swiveling radar operated Gatling gun that shoots 20x102mm rounds faster than you can differentiate the individual rounds. It looks like R2-D2 from the Star Wars movies. These weapons systems are strategically placed around the ship for close in anti-missile, anti-air, or anti-surface threats. All of this display of the *Saratoga*'s power occasionally demonstrated before the crew had the effect of bolstering our confidence and dedication to the cause of freedom of the seas. For those interested, You Tube has videos shot from an aircraft carrier demonstrating the Sea-Wiz firing live rounds and Navy aircraft breaking the sound barrier.

As our eight-month deployment stretched from weeks into passing months, most of the crew were counting the days until we would be home again. I remember a particularly inspirational saying written by some unknown OS or operations officer on one of the many tactical display grease boards where we regularly plotted the bearings, ranges, courses, and speeds of surface contacts in CIC. The nugget of wisdom didn't take up much room on the grease board, but it said so much that we needed to hear. It read: "REMEMBER...This, too, Shall Pass!"

The saying remained on the grease board for the last two months of our eight-month deployment which had been extended beyond the six-month mark due to the Libyan line-of-death operations. It would remain on the grease board until we pulled back into Mayport, Florida in April 16, 1986. I still wonder who wrote that one? It wasn't me. It may have been Captain Unruh; who knows? Though the prophecy was ultimately fulfilled, it seemed at times like we might be at sea forever.

There were certainly tinges of excitement that we had experienced in tense and significant moments that extended, sometimes, into hours and days. There were exotic ports of call with adventures, or disasters, to be experienced by sailors who were eager to put their civilian-shod feet on dry-land. There was always the mysterious and powerful effect of the sea, itself, that rewarded any soul willing to make the short walk to one of the exposed weather decks for a quiet moment and a breathtaking view. In reality, though, one day was much like the next. Due to the geographical distance from our ordinary concerns, missed opportunities, and routine responsibilities back home, it was difficult to extinguish the feeling that you were missing out on something.

Upon our return to homeport, I would still have at least a year left to serve on the *Saratoga* before I fulfilled my three-year active duty obligation to the Navy. Beyond that milestone, I was obligated to continue on with two more years of reserve duty where I would drill one weekend every month at the Navy Reserve facility most convenient to my chosen residence and location. In addition to the weekend-warrior status of a reservist (one weekend a month), you typically have a two-week active duty training once every year, usually in the summer. But reserve duty sounded like a walk in the park, and with just over a year to go before I finished my active duty, I began to feel like I was well over the hump.

For most sailors, returning home from a long deployment induces a euphoric sense of freedom, at least initially. Of course, for many, problems left behind sometimes become compounded, and the strains of deployment upon families can be particularly difficult. For me, a young single guy of nineteen years with aspirations of college and a growing sense of call to the gospel ministry, the future was calling loudly. While underway, there had been opportunities for college credits through the Navy's PACE (Program for Afloat College Education), of which I had taken advantage. I earned three semester hours for English Composition 101 and three more semester hours for General Psychology. It seems the experience of travel overseas had given birth to an intellectual curiosity within me, particularly with regard to the various people groups and languages spoken by the nationalities we encountered in our European ports of call. Where did these people come from? Why are their languages different from one another? What about the various genetic characteristics? I truly wished that I had paid closer attention to my history classes at Independence High School. Add to that the mystique of our port visit to the Holy Land, the transit through the Suez Canal, going through the Indian Ocean to Singapore and other stops along the way, I clearly had more questions than answers.

Greater than merely an intellectual curiosity, I had a growing and distinct sense of call that my life was to be about sharing the gospel of Jesus Christ and serving the purposes of God. Though I did not know what form of ministry related vocation I would pursue at that point; I had a burning desire to tell people about Jesus and, specifically, what He had done for me. In short, I wanted others to find the relationship with Christ that I had recently discovered. I realized, intuitively, that I needed to sharpen my understanding of the world in order to prepare myself for the ministry.

All during the cruise, I had pored over the large red leather-bound King James version of the Bible that I had purchased before our deployment. And this was no ordinary edition of the Bible! I had come across a *Spiros Zodhiates Hebrew-Greek Edition* of the Bible that I had picked up in a Christian Book Store before deployment. Spiros Zodhiates, a Greek American Bible scholar, had meticulously overseen this edition of the Bible which had all of the key words in the English version of the Old Testament underlined and correlated with an index of the corresponding Hebrew words from which the English version had been translated. Also provided were the pronunciations and the definitions of these key words so important to understanding the meaning of the text.

This Hebrew-Greek Key Word Study Bible also included the key words of the English New Testament and the corresponding Greek words from which the English words were translated. These Greek words were offered with relevant information such as definition, pronunciation, and part of speech. I probably spent more time reading the Bible in those days while deployed than I ever have since, but "for everything there is a season" as Scripture says. My time on the *Saratoga* was a season of establishing a firm foundation in the Word of God. It was an extra blessing that I had been able to familiarize myself with the Hebrew and Greek Bible backgrounds, which I would study more formally in Master of Divinity and Ph.D. programs, later when I attended seminary. Remember my earlier confession, that I was the guy whose mother told my high school principal that he should be ashamed for letting me graduate from high school, and she was right. And that was barely a year before I was teaching myself Hebrew and Greek so that I could understand better what the Bible teaches. I am still amazed at the many ways this cruise was a gamechanger for me personally. More accurately put: I am still amazed at the many ways that God can change a person's life when that person is willing!

It did not escape my observation, either, that the privileges enjoyed by officers in the United States Navy were bestowed upon them, it appeared, because of their education. After all, the primary mark of distinction between officers and enlisted persons in the military, when it was all boiled down, seemed to be a college degree. As the cruise of the *Saratoga* began to wind down and I began to think ahead toward my future, college increasingly seemed to be a destination to which I was now charting my course. Increasingly for me, the flight ops that were gaining my attention had more to do with life after the Navy than with what was being catapulted off the flight deck of the *Saratoga*. In other words, I was really feeling ready to launch from the flight deck of the Navy and soar into my future as a civilian!

In the service, this focus forward and readiness to leave the military is called "short-timer's disease." My hopes and dreams were drawing me forward and my flight would soon be away from active duty on an aircraft carrier and on to college admissions. By the time we were preparing to transit back to Mayport from the Mediterranean Sea, I was fairly certain that I would separate from the Navy in just a little over a year's time.

The one regret I had was that I never had another opportunity to take the Navy SEALS fitness test for orders to Basic Underwater Demolition Seal School (BUD/S). In Boot Camp, our company was deprived of our single opportunity to undergo the screening that was offered once every eight-week cycle in boot camp at that time. While it may have just been a fantasy, my fitness level was good, and my mindset was strong as well. I had spent many hours running and swimming in OS "A" School with a fellow student who had taken and passed the screening test in Boot Camp. I had watched with some envy when Flynn shipped out for the Naval Special Warfare Center in Coronado, California for Bud/S after graduation from OS "A" School.

My life had taken a different course after "A" School leading me to the aircraft carrier *Saratoga* stationed in Mayport, Florida. This divinely ordered path had put me exactly where it seemed that God had planned for me to be. My life had changed remarkably. I had experienced many things. A call to the ministry was beginning to emerge in my heart with greater intensity, even though the specifics were not clear to me at that time. Yet, the desire to pursue, or at least, an attempt to gain entrance into the Seal Teams lingered in my mind. I knew that if I did not try to open the door I would have regrets later. I began to research the option. I was told that I would have to commit to an extension of my enlistment for a full five years beyond graduation from BUD/S, which took six months itself. Basically, I would have to add another five years of time, at minimum, to the 15 months remaining on my enlistment. That was not something that I was willing to do.

My thinking and my growing sense of call to follow Christ into the ministry had changed me as a person during our deployment. When aircraft from the *Saratoga* engaged and struck the Nanunchka Class Libyan Vessels with immediate death-toll results, cheering arose in CIC. It struck me, however, that these who were killed in action were simply young men like me who had joined the Navy. The leader of these young sailors, Muammar Gaddafi, had committed them to a course of direct conflict with the United States. The sailors on the Libyan ships we had taken action against were simply following orders and they were caught up in this Cold War proxy contest.

Like my shipmates, I had no misgivings about our response to the Libyan line-of-death provocations or our use of overwhelming force in response to Libya's firing of missiles upon our battle group. What struck me as saddening was the mindset of cheering while persons were dying as a result of our collective efforts to meet fire with fire. Almost all of the people in CIC had trained months and years for just such an occasion, so that their enthusiasm in applying their knowledge and training is understandable. Truthfully, it is likely that few in the room gave much thought to the loss of life on the other side. We, in CIC, were just caught in the rare moment of armed naval combat. Even *Saratoga*'s Commanding Officer at the time, Captain Jerry Unruh, recently told me that beyond this occasion he had never been in a live General Quarters situation onboard a ship in his thirty-seven years in the Navy. Undoubtedly, the action taken against Libya by the *Saratoga* Battle Group was a big deal.

As I reflected on it all in the minutes immediately following these incidents, it occurred to me that I was becoming a different person with a different calling upon my life. With just a little over a year left in the Navy, I had to determine if I were going to throw away my dream of going to BUD/S or not. I was only nineteen at the time, so I thought I had time in my life to do the SEAL thing and then pursue the call to ministry. The Libyan Conflict, and specifically my lack of ease with the cheering over the live fire and loss of life, was causing me to doubt whether I was of the mindset to function within the SEAL Teams due to the nature of their work as assaulters, snipers, and demolition experts.

What did I do? I sought out a half-way measure which I thought might fulfill my desire for greater excitement in the Navy during my final year of active duty enlistment. The plan I was hatching might also allow me to avoid the five-year extension, and possible conflicts of conscience that I suspected active duty service with the Navy SEALS might bring. I don't remember if it was during the latter days of the cruise or after we had returned to Mayport, but I walked down to the Explosive Ordinance Disposal (EOD) locker to speak with a Chief about the possibility of my pursuit of EOD training. I figured that since EOD got to scuba dive, wear cool wet suits, and carry a dive-knife it might be the perfect short-term path to further adventure for me. In addition, EODs were trained for any contingency, so guns were involved, but they generally kept people from being blown up – as opposed to blowing people up. Perfect!

I asked myself the question, "What Would Jesus Do?" (WWJD). Jesus would not want people to be blown up, and in the EOD, you are disposing of things that blow people up. This might be the right thing! Wasn't that the point with Christ's going to the cross to die for our sins anyway? Hadn't he jeopardized his life to save others? Doesn't Jesus want us to dispose of the destructive things that are harmful to ourselves and others - physically and spiritually harmful - that is? You can see how my thinking was evolving as a young man increasingly conscious of a higher call to represent the kingdom of God; yet I still had my own hopes and dreams to consider.

Well, of course, Jesus would join the Explosive Ordinance Disposal unit, right? It seemed logical and potentially satisfying at the time. Well, I can tell you the EOD Chief on the *Saratoga* was not too enthused about my half-hearted interest evidenced by my probing questions about minimal obligation time in EOD service and the like. Consequently, the EOD Chief sent me walking that day and it was increasingly apparent that God was closing the doors on any remaining interest in staying in the Navy to pursue my personal ambitions.

After a typical ten-day transit back across the Atlantic Ocean eventually bearing southwest toward Mayport, Florida, it was almost difficult to grasp that the deployment was coming to an end. I don't remember all the feelings that I felt but, suffice it to say, coming home itself was a game changer. As we pulled into the St. Johns river and arrived at Mayport Naval Station, *Saratoga* sailors in their dress whites manned the rails and we received an epic welcome home. Red, White, and Blue helium-filled balloons, too many to count, were released into the air as music played and the Jacksonville Bulls Cheerleaders, from the U.S.F.L. Professional Football League, cheered us wildly. Throngs of people including wives, children, girlfriends, and others stood eagerly waiting to see loved ones they had rarely spoken with, and had not seen, for eight months. There were first-time fathers coming home to see children who had been born during the deployment.

My brothers in Christ from the Maranatha Christian Servicemen's Center in nearby Atlantic Beach had said they would be there to welcome me upon my arrival. Sure enough, there they stood with Don Kalina, their spiritual leader, who had truly been a factor in my turn around during those first few months onboard *Saratoga* before our deployment. After our port visit to Singapore at Christmas, I had written Don to let him know that I felt the Lord was leading me back toward my Baptist spiritual roots, but that I would always be in his debt for the influence he, a charismatic pastor, had upon my life. It was a bit awkward, but I hugged Don and each one of the half dozen or so brothers from the Center. We exchanged some banter about the military events that had been carried in the news regarding the *Saratoga*. That was pretty much it. I told Don that I had to catch a ride with a shipmate back to Charlotte to see my family, and I turned to make my way through the frenzied crowd.

Much had happened in eight months, and that's an understatement. Yes, we had captured the terrorists who hijacked the *Achille Lauro*. We had taken part in the largest sea-battle since World War II. Our battle group had been fired upon, and we had responded. No American lives were lost in that action, but lives had been taken. With regard to the larger context, our Commander in Chief, Ronald Reagan, had used strong persuasion to lead the Soviet Union's Mikhail Gorbachev into a game changing political and economic policy shift, called *Perestroika*.

By the time of *Saratoga*'s return, Gorbachev had found it necessary to negotiate from a position of weakness relative to the United States as we had outpaced them economically and militarily over the previous half dozen years. Barely a year past the *Saratoga*'s return from her eventful Med/IO deployment, on June 12, 1987, President Reagan would stand in front of the Brandenburg Gate, just feet from the infamous Berlin Wall, to confidently utter the words: "Mr. Gorbachev, tear down this wall!"[34]

The full dissolution of the Soviet Union would not officially take place until December 26, 1991; but the Cold War was for all practical purposes nearly over. The first was Poland, in 1989, then one by one, the client nation-states under the Communist regime in Moscow declared their political freedom. The world was rapidly changing, and it is no leap of faith to acknowledge that the 1985-86 deployment of the aircraft carrier *Saratoga* had played a significant role in moving the ball forward.

On a personal level, I had developed as an Operations Specialist during our deployment, making Third Class Petty Officer. I had reversed an eighteen-year academic slump characterized by disinterest in learning and had filled that void with an awakening of the mind and a budding curiosity over nearly everything. As I said above, I had even managed to earn six semester hours of college credit while deployed, with two core courses under my belt. Granted, it wasn't much. But it was a start, and best of all, it had cost me nothing! Thank-you Uncle Sam!

More importantly, I was a different person because of what the LORD had done in my life during our deployment. I had surrendered my will to the Holy Spirit of God. I had been baptized in the River Jordan by a Navy Chaplain along with over a hundred of my shipmates. I had the beginnings of a consistent call to the gospel ministry that would propel me forward to do my best at everything for the glory of God. My time on the *Saratoga* had been a game changer that seemed to be part of God's unfolding plan for my life. As the Scripture says: "God's ways are higher than our ways," and "He is able to do exceedingly abundantly above all that we think or ask." To Him be the glory!

CHAPTER 13

FROM THE CAPTAIN'S BRIDGE: HIGHLIGHTS FROM VICE ADMIRAL JERRY L. UNRUH

The *Saratoga* was operating in the Western Mediterranean, more than 900 miles to the West of Egypt, when we were notified of the hijacking of the *Achille Lauro*. We immediately began the trek to the eastern Med while flying long range surveillance, searching for the cruise ship. Once the ship was located, we maintained 24-hour covert surveillance while the National Command authority formed the special operations team that would carry out the assigned mission. The plan came together quickly, which was to take down the high-jacked ship with Navy Seals. Two Air Force C-141 Aircraft would fly the special operators in, where they would be supported by US Army personnel providing satellite communications and *Saratoga* would provide surveillance and fighter cover while the Seals would make a late night low-level jump onto the deck of the cruise ship and capture the terrorists in close combat, striving for minimum civilian casualties.

Due to the circumstances, the planning called for a good number of Seals to parachute onto the *Achille Lauro*, knowing that some would be successful but others would likely miss their target dropping into the dark ocean. The *Saratoga* would later find and recover them.

In the late afternoon hours before the midnight raid, the terrorists left the ship via high speed boats that Abu Abbas had arranged. Once departure from the cruise ship was verified, *Saratoga* was released to proceed to a scheduled port visit in Dubrovnik, Yugoslavia. About 18 hours later as Saratoga was entering the Ionian Sea, without warning, we were directed to immediately launch fighters and the E-2C Surveillance/airborne command and control aircraft, mission to be provided. The mission, find the Egyptian airliner flying the terrorists to Tunisia and force them down. No rules of engagement were given to us, we were to use our best judgement. Given the first sketchy intelligence, we sent the fighters direct towards Tunis, Tunisia, in hopes of intercepting their plane before landing.

Subsequent information made us skeptical of the flight takeoff time and from that point for extended hours, multiple F-14 Tomcats, flying lights out and silent, intercepted every airliner flying over the Mediterranean Sea, joining on each one, flying up underneath in the dark moonless sky and looking for Egypt Air markings on a Boeing 737. The operation was conducted covertly without the international air traffic control being aware and the pilots of the intercepted airliners never knowing they were being intercepted. The Navy pilots performed superbly.

During the operation, President Reagan wanted updates on the search effort and periodic voice exchanges were conducted directly with the White House. It was a difficult task and probability of success was questionable. When *Saratoga* was asked what could the White House do to assist, we offered a cancellation of the flight clearance to land in Tunis would be helpful. That in fact did happen and played a part in the capture. When one of the Tomcat crews found the suspect airliner, they flew extremely close, up under the tail, and with flashlights they read the serial number of the plane on the underbelly. It matched, confirming that the terrorists and Abu Abbas were on board. With four Tomcats surrounding the airliner, heavily armed with missiles, the Egyptian Airline pilot reluctantly agreed to comply with the demand to divert to a NATO base in Sicily. Tomcats flew his wing and on his second attempt at landing at an unfamiliar mountainous airport, he landed safely. Then, from behind the mountains, the two US Air Force C-141's popped up and landed behind the airliner, blocking the runway and out came the Navy Seals to apprehend the terrorists.

NIGHT TRANSIT OF THE SUEZ CANAL/LONG RANGE STRIKE/DIEGO GARCIA DOCKING/ SINGAPORE CHRISTMAS VISIT/GULF OF SIDRA-GENERAL QUARTERS

Following the action-filled first half of *Saratoga*'s deployment, Commander in Chief, U.S. Pacific fleet recognized her precedent setting level of combat readiness as he modified schedules for the various underway battle groups. It would seem he was taking advantage of our capabilities. As he laid on more requirements, the USS *Saratoga* was being stressed but the "Mighty Fine" crew fulfilled all tasking with great success. The decision was made to keep the aircraft carrier USS *Coral Sea* in the Mediterranean and instead send *Saratoga* on to the Indian Ocean in her place. Egypt was embarrassed by our earlier successful force-down of the Egypt Air flight carrying the terrorists and would not approve the *Saratoga* transit of the Suez Canal. After much diplomatic negotiation, we were approved to transit but it had to be in the dark of night. That had never been done before by a super carrier of our size, lighted channel markers were very limited, and there were portions of the canal that were unsafe due to the narrowness of full depth water – as little as 110 yards wide.

The Egyptian Canal Pilot was unfamiliar with guiding a super carrier where the bridge is not the centerline of the ship but rather on the extreme right side. Without the *Saratoga* Commanding Officer giving repeated assistance, this first night transit, a 10-hour evolution, would have been a disaster. The watch teams and navigation crew performed superbly.

On completion of the Suez passage and upon entering the Red Sea, the Fleet Commander sent tasking requiring the airwing to plan and execute for training a large force "Alpha Strike," to demonstrate our capability to aerial refuel and deliver bombs to targets 1,500 miles distant and return to the carrier – a 3,000 mile round trip. The event would stretch the aerial refueling requirements for the mission aircraft to our very limit.

As we steamed out of the Gulf of Aden the execute order was received and the launch began. Aircrews would be flying a 10- hour mission reaching deep into the Indian Ocean. The airwing/ship team performed flawlessly and all aircraft returned successfully. On entering the Indian Ocean, the *Saratoga* Battle Group took on certain contingencies requiring a readiness to support actions against rogue nations. Our strike demonstration facilitated our being able to stretch our operations enough to make a port visit to Singapore to celebrate Christmas. Additionally, *Saratoga* and her accompanying battle group ships had the pleasure of a celebration picnic on the beautiful beaches of the island Diego Garcia.

Saratoga's port of call to Diego Garcia was made possible by the carrier docking at the pier built for carriers there in the lagoon. The *Saratoga* Captain, proficient in ship handling, brought the ship in to the pier when it became obvious the assigned harbor pilot was incapable. No large aircraft carriers had ever attempted to dock there before and the Fleet Commander wanted to prove the capability and further enhance logistical support for deployed forces. Following a full review of the evolution it was deemed too risky for aircraft carriers of our size due to shoal waters, limited maneuvering room and the prevailing winds and cross-currents. Thus the "Mighty Fine" carrier *Saratoga* remains unique in its accomplishment!

LIBYAN OPERATIONS/GULF OF SIDRA/GENERAL QUARTERS

As USS *Saratoga*'s deployment was reaching its final months before returning to Jacksonville, Florida and the big homecoming celebration for the crew and their families, the Fleet Commander had one more major task for us. Libyan President Moammar Kaddafi was becoming increasingly more belligerent, claiming the Mediterranean waters, 200 miles out to sea as his territorial waters. International shipping and particularly the US Navy were to ask his permission to transit. He considered the Gulf of Sidra, a very large open body of water as his, prohibiting entrance. His claims were not recognized by most nations in the world. International agreements specify 12 miles as the accepted limit of territorial waters. Likewise, he also claimed the airspace above these waters. Five years earlier Libyan jets had challenged US fighters for the airspace and the Libyan jets were shot down. The Libyan fighter aircraft once again were more aggressive and Libyan surface-to-surface missile firing ships (of Soviet origin) were guarding Libya's claims.

Proceeding back to the Med in order to address the Libyan situation, *Saratoga* once again transited the Suez Canal. Unlike our previous transit, this time was a pleasurable daytime picture taking trip. Once in the Med, however, the *Saratoga* Battle Group was assisted by aircraft from two more carriers in the area. The *Saratoga* would be the flag ship of a three-carrier battle group including the USS *America* and the USS *Coral Sea*. Together, we would soon deliver a solid blow to the Libyan threats of violence and military action.

On orders from the US National Command Authority, President Reagan, his secretaries of State and Defense, US forces, led by the *Saratoga* Battle Group, on 23 March 1986 crossed Kaddafi's "Line of Death" and the fight was on. Libya responded with high speed missile ships and land-based missiles. Hostilities commenced when Libyan missile sites fired SA-5's (latest Soviet surface to air missiles) at Saratoga F-14 Tomcats outside the 12-mile territorial waters limit.

The designated commander responsible for the sea engagements was the Commanding Officer, USS *Saratoga*. He reported to the on-board Battle Group Admiral. On board to observe the operation was the Mediterranean Fleet Commander. During the at-sea engagements, late into the night, at the moment the last wave of strike aircraft departed and transited deep into the gulf, and the recovering aircraft had just landed, locking the deck for re-spot and re-arm, a US ship from one of the other carrier groups reported that a Libyan missile boat had apparently slipped out of an unknown port and escaped to the North and now coming South to shoot *Saratoga*.

The crew had been conditioned for this possibility and as the Captain called General Quarters, all hands raced to their battle stations. The Captain called for maximum power and turned the carrier South for time to assess the developing situation. His superiors pressed him to shoot a surface-to-surface Harpoon missile at the attacker. Without full identity of the target he refused to fire, even though the ship was potentially in imminent danger. Racing to the bridge, he ordered a helicopter to go lights out, low to the water and proceed forward in order to identify the target. He was putting the pilots in the surface-to-air missile envelope, with hopes of them not being lost. The pilots risked their lives but reported back – "Don't shoot, it is a civilian Cruise ship passing thru the area." Once again, *Saratoga*'s ship/airwing team won the day. Three attacking Libyan missile boats were left burning on the water, the land missile site was destroyed and their radar command center and facilities bombed to destruction. The operation was complete in less than 24 hours and in the brief encounter, US forces suffered no casualties, no injuries, and no damage.

Vice Admiral Jerry L. Unruh, USN (ret)
21 Sep 2019

AFTERWORD

TO THE HORIZON & BACK

Looking back to events that took place thirty to forty years previous is an interesting endeavor, especially when these events seem, in retrospect, to be so formative. As one who did not grow up planning to join the military, it is surprising that the experience occurred, and much more that it was so significant in terms of shaping my life.

The navy's recruiting slogan in the mid-1980's: "**NAVY – *it's not just a job; its an adventure***" pretty well sums up my experience during that time. And fortunately, the adventures didn't stop when my time in the navy ended. I met my wife, Elyse, on a mission trip to Mombasa, Kenya in the summer of 1990, while I was in between my junior and senior year at the University of North Carolina at Greensboro, and serving the Florida Street Baptist Church as its Youth Minister. Elyse and I married a year later in the summer of 1991. After eight years of marriage, and two graduate seminary degrees, we had our first-born son, Garrison, in Columbia, South Carolina in year 2000. While serving as South Carolina Baptist Convention's Director of Evangelism & Missions, I took a mission trip to Beirut, Lebanon later that year, in the summer of 2000. There I saw a precious baby-boy, Joseph, in an orphanage, and we adopted him, bringing our count of sons to two – only eleven weeks apart in age.

When the boys were just over a year-old, on September 11, 2001, our nation was suddenly struck by the Al Qaida Terrorist Network, resulting in 2,977 deaths and 6,000 others were injured. Like everyone else who was alive; I remember where I was that day. At 9:30am, I was speaking to a group of pastors from the Pickens Baptist Association at the East Pickens Baptist Church on that fateful Tuesday morning. The pastor of the church, Carl Martin, was host. I was there to give instruction and inspiration to pastors with regard to sharing their faith in Jesus Christ with others. Jeff Wright, Carl's Student Minister, suddenly interrupted the meeting and said that commercial airplanes had flown into the Twin Towers in NY, and it looked like a terrorist attack.

I was occupying the pulpit as the featured speaker with the eyes of about thirty to forty pastors of local churches looking at me as if to say: "What do we do now?" My immediate thought, which I put into words, was: "Dear brothers, life as we have known it has just changed forever." Time has thus far proven my words to be accurate. We stand in long lines for airport security. If we watch the news, we do so, hoping no act of violence has taken place this day as a result of the war on terror. Our schools, churches, malls, and public gatherings march on, but with an air of suspicion and vigilance. Perhaps, even more disturbing, is the increase in incidents of gun violence, some of which have been random acts with various motivations.

I quickly wrapped up my talk at the East Pickens Baptist Church, closed in prayer for our nation, for those in peril at the scene of the hostilities, and dashed to my car for the two-hour drive from

Pickens to Lexington, South Carolina. I wanted to be with my wife and my two sons. National news coverage of the events that morning evidenced the severity of the attacks, of which there had been three different ones that morning, and no one knew if, or when, the next strike would occur.

After I got home that day, more information about the acts of terror were forthcoming. In the days immediately following Tuesday morning September the 11th, an armed services recruitment drive was broadcast on local television in Columbia, South Carolina. I called to see about joining up but could not get through the busy phone lines. It seemed to me that we were at war, and the only place for me was to be with those protecting our families and our nation.

Over the next few years, the intensity of the conflict would ebb and flow, but there is no doubt that we were on a defensive war footing as threats continued to emanate from Osama ben Laden and other emerging jihadist leaders in the Middle East and North Africa. Somewhere along the way, in those early years after 9-11, I made contact with a Navy recruiter and expressed my interest in going back in as a Navy chaplain. A female officer whose job it was to recruit medical doctors and chaplains for the Navy drove from Charleston, SC to my home in Lexington to meet with me about military service in the Navy Chaplain Corps. As she sat in our den, with Elyse and our two toddlers playing on the floor near us, the Navy Lieutenant confessed that she was new in her recruiting job and had no idea about the formalities of recruiting a Navy chaplain.

Perhaps that is why I was completely dropped through the cracks and my willingness to volunteer, once again, had been met with a closed door. First, immediately after 9-11, when I couldn't get a call through to the military recruiting telethon. And now, once again, when a recruiting officer had even driven two hours to my front door, all of the doors, for me, seemed to be tightly closed. With a national climate of war and a growing sense of dissatisfaction with my convention job, I even began to explore employment with the Central Intelligence Agency in Langley, Virginia, but entry level field service jobs didn't seem to offer sufficient pay to support a family of four, and I just couldn't arrive at a sense of peace about the idea.

About that time, in 2003, several churches around the country began to express interest in my resume, and I concluded that God had closed the doors on any future military service in my lifetime. The war on terror had become an unfortunate routine in our nation and the urgency seemed to be mostly behind us. After several months of searching for God's direction, we ultimately responded to the invitation to move to the Atlanta-area, where I became the fourth senior pastor of Briarlake Baptist Church in Decatur, Georgia in September of 2004. I was thirty-eight years old at the time and the church happily welcomed our young family. We had a third son, Bailey, in 2005 and the years have flown.

When I look back upon my adventures with the *Saratoga*, I am grateful to God for what occurred in my life during those formative years. It is my hope that the telling of my story will attest to the goodness of God and His ability to do great things though human lives in the midst of challenging circumstances. Maybe there is a young sailor on a ship at sea who is praying? Perhaps there is a parent of a teen with no direction in life who may take courage from this story? Wouldn't it be wonderful if our nation saw a spiritual awakening, like we had on the *Saratoga*, where lives were changed, races were reconciled, and new-found successes achieved? If I've learned anything, it is that God is full of surprises and He knows exactly what He is doing! All the best...

ENDNOTES

A quick word about sources and documentation: I chose to go sparsely on documentation since nearly everything can be verified with a few quick keystrokes on a smart phone. Wishing for GAME CHANGER to feel more like informative pleasure reading than academic study, my documented references will be scarce, and only included when I think it is preferable to note them.

Introduction

1 Haney, Eric L. 2002. *Inside Delta Force: The Story of America's Elite Counterterrorist Unit*. New York: Delacorte Press, from the book back cover.

2 Captain Hugo S. Hammond, USN (ret), phone conversation, September 9, 2019.

Chapter 1

3 Matthew 28:18-20.

4 Romans 6:1-4.

Chapter 2

5 There is a wealth of sources in various media reports on the Saratoga's involvement with the Achille Lauro Affair. I will cite

one primary source, a CIA released doc, which is included in my select bibliography. *You Can Run but You Can't Hide: The terrorists who highjacked the Achille Lauro fall into an audacious trap.* Sanitized copy approved for release 04 March 2011.

6 Abramson, Rudy. No *Apology for Capture, Reagan Says 'Never,' He Replies on Regrets Over Forcing Down Jet.* LA Times. October 16, 1985.

Chapter 3

7 West, Diana. 2013. *American Betrayal: The Secret Assault on Our Nation's Character.* New York: St. Martin's Griffin. P.54. In this interesting book, the author asserts, among several things, that our national leadership has long been reluctant to hold the Soviet Union accountable for its atrocities. She rightly points out that the Soviet Union also invaded Poland in 1939, along with Adolph Hitler. At that time, the Nazis and the Communists were in alliance. Her conclusion is that we stick it to the Nazis, and we should, while we whitewash the aggressions of Communists and Islamic terrorists, which we shouldn't. All of this makes for interesting reading.

8 West, Diana. 2013. American Betrayal: *The Secret Assault on Our Nation's Character.* New York: St. Martin's Griffin. In pages 1-6, the author meticulously recounts a Democratic-led congressional cover-up of communist penetration of the US government in the year 1934. In pages 43-45, she recounts the preferential treatment that the Soviet military, and the Soviet Union as a whole, received from the Lend-Lease Program, through which the United States government supplied the soviets with everything from food to armaments. Examples of the generosity of the US government towards the soviets include a whopping 217,660,666 pounds of

butter sent to the Soviet Union, while Americans were suffering strict rationing and often going without such things back in the USA. Even Soviet Air Force was better supplied by the US government than was the US Air Force, as per testimony given to Congress during hearings to assess the extent of the communist penetration of the US government in 1949.

Chapter 4

9 Mattson, Kevin. 2018. *What the Heck Are You Up to Mr. President? Jimmy Carter, America's "Malaise," and the Speech that Should Have Changed the Country.*

10 Pederson, Dan. 2019. *TOP GUN: An American Story*. New York: Hachette Books, 262.

Chapter 5

11 Siceloff, Bruce. *Second to None,* NC *now offers choice of* 2 *'First' license plates.* News-Observer. *July* 01, 2015.

12 Seelye, Katherine Q. and Jeff Zeleny. *On the Defensive, Obama Calls His Words Ill-Chosen.* New York Times. April 13, 2008.

13 Wallis, Michael. 2011. *David Crockett: The Lion of the West.* New York: W.W. Norton. In his introduction, Wallis gives testament to the exploding interest in Davy Crockett from the introduction of the historic character to tv audiences in 1954. $100 million dollars would be spent on Crockett merchandise in the following year. Baby-boomers gobbled it up. Though I was born in 1966, it is obvious that the phenomenon lingered on, at least in my imagination.

14 1 Corinthians 2:14, et. al.

Chapter 7

15 Read John chapter 3 for the well-known quote of Jesus in its full context.

Chapter 8

16 Haney, *Inside Delta Force*, Back Cover quote.

17 Feltman, Jeffrey. *Hezbollah: Revolutionary Iran's Most Successful Export*. January 17, 2019. Brookings.edu.

18 Ephesians 1:4-5; 13-14

Chapter 9

19 Luke 22:39-44

20 Hebrews 9:22

21 Isaiah 53:4-5

22 Galatians 4:4-6

23 2 Corinthians 5:19

Chapter 10

24 James 1:5-8

25 Romans 8:9

26 Skinner, Betty, with a foreword by Billy Graham. 1998. *Daws: A Man Who Trusted God*. Colorado Springs: NavPress.

27 2 Timothy 3:14-17

Chapter 11

28 John 8:20 & 8:59

29 Hebrews 13:4, Genesis 2:24-25, Matthew 19:4-6, Ephesians 5:22-33

30 Genesis 39

31 1 Corinthians 10:23-33

32 There are a good number of books recounting the specific history and details of Christian spiritual awakenings. My clear favorite is Arnold Dallimore's two-volume collection recounting the famed English-evangelist George Whitefield, who conspicuously led the First Great Awakening in America during the decades of the early 18th century. This revival movement was the first newsworthy inter-colonial movement in the early American colonies and historians claim that it gave rise to our Independence Movement from the British in 1776. It is definitely good reading! Arnold Dallimore. 1980. *George Whitefield: The Life and Times of the Great Evangelist of the Eighteenth Century -vols. 1 &2*. Carlisle, PA: Banner of Truth Publishing.

Chapter 12

33 Harrington, Rebecca. 2016. *Here's what happens during a sonic boom...* Business Insider. January 28, 2016.

34 A good number of official Soviet government documents reveal the degree to which the Soviet Union feared and respected President Ronald Reagan, the American Commander in Chief, during the years 1981-1989. One of these document collections is by: Andrew, Christopher, and Oleg Gordievsky. *Comrade Kryuchko's Instructions: Top Secret Files on KGB Foreign Operations*, 1975-85. Stanford, CA: Stanford University Press, 1993. Reagan's commitment to victory over Soviet Communism is well documented in Peter Schweizer's work entitled: *Reagan's War: The Epic Story of His Forty-Year Struggle and Final Triumph Over Communism.* 2002. New York: Doubleday. Numerous times, during phone conversations, as well as in text and email correspondence, Admiral Jerry Unruh expressed his great admiration for Ronald Reagan as Commander in Chief. In

addition, Admiral Unruh referenced several times of his experience in direct talks with the Reagan White House and Situation Room during Saratoga's engagements with the Achille Lauro Terrorists.

SELECT BIBLIOGRAPHY

Andrew, Christopher, and Oleg Gordievsky. 1993. *Comrade Kryuchkov's Instructions: Top Secret Files on KGB Foreign Operations,* 1975-85. Stanford, CA: Stanford University Press.

Andrew, Christopher, and Vasili Mitrokhin. 1999. *The Sword and The Shield: The Mitrokhin Archive and the Secret History of the* KGB. New York: Basic Books.

Balmer, Randall. 2016. *Evangelicals in America.* Waco: Baylor University Press.

Central Intelligence Agency. Sanitized Copy Approved for Release on 04 MARCH 2011. "You Can Run but You Can't Hide": The terrorists who highjacked the Achille Lauro fall into an audacious trap. CIA-RDP91-00587R000100080005-0.

Coll, Steve. 2004. *Ghost Wars: The Secret History of the CIA, Afghanistan, and Bin Laden, From the Soviet Invasion to September 10,* 2001. New York: The Penguin Press.

Dallimore, Arnold. 1970 & 1980 respectively. *George Whitefield: The*

Life and Times of the Great Evangelist of the Eighteenth Century – vols. 1&2. Carlisle, PA: Banner of Truth Publishing.

Freeman, Gregory A. 2004. *Sailors to the End: The Deadly Fire on the USS Forrestal and the Heroes Who Fought It*. New York: William Morrow Paperbacks.

Haney, Eric L. 2002. *Inside Delta Force: The Story of America's Elite Counterterrorist Unit*. New York: Delacorte Press.

Homer, and Emily Wilson, translator. 2018. *The Odyssey*. New York: W.W. Norton & Company.

Kelly, Orr. 1992. *Brave Men Dark Waters: The Untold Story of the Navy Seals*. New York: Presidio Press.

Macintyre, Ben. 2018. *The Spy and The Traitor: The Greatest Espionage Story of the Cold War*. New York: Crown.

Marcinko, Richard, and John Weisman. 1993. ROGUE WARRIOR: *The Explosive Autobiography of the Controversial Founder of the US Navy's Seal Team Six*. New York: Pocket Books.

Marx, Karl, and Frederick Engels. 1998. *The Communist Manifesto: A Modern Edition*. London: Verso.

Matlock, Jr. Jack F. 2004. *Reagan and Gorbachev: How the Cold War Ended*. New York: Random House.

Mattson, Kevin. 2009. *What the Heck Are You Up To, Mr. President:*

Jimmy Carter, America's "Malaise," and the Speech that Should Have Changed the Country. New York: Bloomsbury USA.

McDowell, Josh, and Sean McDowell. 2017. *Evidence That Demands a Verdict*. Nashville: Thomas Nelson.

Morrow, William. 2018. *A Prophet with Honor: The Billy Graham Story*. Grand Rapids: Zondervan.

Pedersen, Dan. 2019. *TOP GUN: An American Story*. New York: Hachette Books.

Skinner, Betty. 1998. *Daws: A Man Who Trusted God*. Colorado Springs: NavPress.

Schweizer, Peter. 2002. *Reagan's War: The Epic Story of His Forty-Year Struggle and Final Triumph Over Communism*. New York: Doubleday.

Tanner, Jane. 1994. *The USS Saratoga: Remembering One of America's Great Aircraft Carriers* 1956-1994. New York: Longstreet Press.

Townley, Alvin. 2011. *FLY NAVY: Discovering the Extraordinary People and Enduring Spirit of Naval Aviation*. New York: St Martin's Press.

Tzu, Sun., and Gary Gagliardi, translator. 2014. *The Art of War*. New York: Clear Bridge Publishing.

USS Saratoga: 30th *Anniversary Edition Cruise Book*, 1985-86.

Wallis, Michael. 2011. *David Crockett: The Lion of The West.* New York: W. W. Norton.

West, Diana. 2013. *American Betrayal: The Secret Assault on Our Nation's Character.* New York: St. Martins Griffin.

Wheen, Francis. 2001. *Karl Marx: A Life.* New York: W. W. Norton & Company.

Wright, Lawrence. 2007. *The Looming Tower:* AL-QAEDA *and The Road to 9/11.* New York: Vintage.

APPENDIX

ARTICLE APPEARED ON PAGE 32

NEWSWEEK
21 October 1985

SPECIAL REPORT

'You Can Run But You Can't Hide'

STAT

The terrorists who hijacked the Achille Lauro fall into an audacious airborne trap.

The mood in the White House basement at 8 o'clock Thursday morning was despondent. The Reagan administration's counterterrorist team ended its first meeting of the day. Egyptian President Hosni Mubarak passed the word to U.S. Ambassador Nicholas Veliotes and repeated it publicly: the hijackers of the Italian cruise ship Achille Lauro had left Egypt. The deal, Mubarak said, was struck with the PLO before the murder of Leon Klinghoffer had come to light. The news appeared to dash the Reagan administration's hope of catching the terrorists. Veliotes had attempted to deliver a cable from the president himself to Mubarak, and Secretary of State George Shultz had tried to telephone the Egyptian president. Mubarak deflected all contact with the Americans to his foreign minister, Esmat Abdel Meguid, and to Defense Minister Abdel Halim Abu Ghazala. As the meeting broke up, one discouraged team member turned to the group's chairman, National Security Council Deputy Staff Director John Poindexter. "It looks like it's all over," Poindexter said.

The American intelligence community, which had kept a close eye on Egypt and the southeastern Mediterranean for signs of the hijackers, lowered the priority of its operations in the area: raw intelligence no longer was being processed immediately, analyzed and fed to top policymakers. Some of the Navy's elite SEAL Team Six were back in Gibraltar, en route home from another fruitless and frustrating wait at the American base at Sigonella, Sicily. But before they threw in the towel, U.S. officials decided to make one more pass at their sources—and just before 8:30 that morning, there was startling news.

One source produced convincing evidence that Mubarak was lying, that the terrorists were still in Egypt and that they probably would try to leave by air. Armed with this information, the NSC's terrorism expert, Marine Lt. Col. Oliver North, a veteran of countless covert operations and the Reagan administration's controversial liaison to the Nicaraguan contras, went to Poindexter and said, "Maybe they really are still there."

On that hope, the U.S. intelligence community plunged back to work trying to confirm the report. Charles Allen, the CIA's national intelligence officer for counterterrorism, ordered the flow of information turned up again. Within an hour Allen reported back that evidence suggested that the four hijackers were still in Egypt and that neither Egypt nor the PLO had figured out what to do with them.

Back at the White House, North had an idea. "Do you remember Yamamoto?" he asked Poindexter, referring to the Japanese admiral whose military transport was intercepted and shot down by American P-38 fighters in the South Pacific during World War II. "God, we can't shoot them down," replied Poindexter. "No, but we have two choices," said North. "Our friends could shoot them down or we can force them down somewhere."

"Where?" Poindexter asked. "Sigonella," replied North. With Poindexter's blessing, North called Vice Adm. Arthur Moreau, the Joint Chiefs of Staff representative on the counterterrorism task force, and told him his idea. Moreau said he would look

F-14 Tomcats on the flight deck of the USS Saratoga: A Navy posse took to the skies

Continued

into it. and within 10 minutes he was back on the line. The Sixth Fleet, he said, could do the job. North, Moreau and a team of Pentagon officers went to work, outlining a plan to intercept the terrorists if they tried to leave Egypt by air. The administration had never written a contingency plan for snatching a civilian jet from the air. "This was somewhat more improvisational than usual," said one insider. "It was just creative thinking."

Other officials grilled the Central Intelligence Agency and National Security Agency on how sure they were of the intelligence they were feeding in a steady stream to the White House Situation Room. At the State Department, Under Secretary for Political Affairs Michael Armacost, aided by Deputy Assistant Secretary for Near Eastern Affairs Arnold Raphel, analyzed the political pros and cons of such a daring move. By late morning, Adm. William J. Crowe, the new chairman of the Joint Chiefs of Staff, was ready to telephone Defense Secretary Caspar Weinberger with the group's preliminary evaluation. "Our boys are good," he reported. "I think they can do it. I think we should let them try."

By 11 o'clock U.S. sources had confirmed that the terrorists were still trying to get out of Egypt. Intelligence sources had located the plane the terrorists planned to use for their getaway: an EgyptAir Boeing 737 jetliner, drawn up on the runway at Al Maza Air Base northeast of Cairo. The spotters reported its identification number and the name of its pilot to Washington. There were signs that the terrorists meant to fly to Tunis. North presented his plan for intercepting them to Poindexter. It called for the launching of the aircraft carrier Saratoga's F-14 jets and radar planes to surprise the terrorists over the Mediterranean, calling the SEAL's back from Gibraltar to Sigonella and forcing the Egyptian plane to land in Sicily.

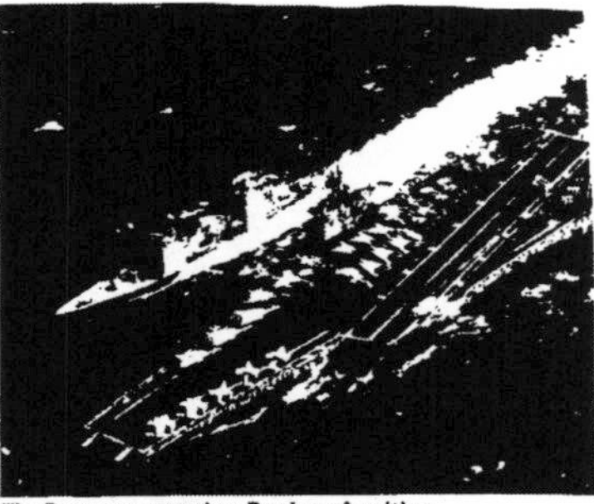
The Saratoga on station: Ready and waiting

ıcking the hijackers as they left Cairo and bringing them to heel

At about 11:30 North sent the design to national-security adviser Robert McFarlane, who was traveling aboard Air Force One to Chicago with President Reagan. North used a secure data communications link (not a phone). The president and White House chief of staff Don Regan had just finished lunch at the Kitchens of Sara Lee outside Chicago. Although McFarlane provided only the broadest outline, Reagan agreed to the idea in principle. The president insisted, however, that he wanted to know more about the risk of casualties before giving his final approval.

McFarlane called Poindexter back and said the president had approved the plan but wanted to see the specifics, including the exact rules of engagement that would govern the U.S. pilots, before he gave the go-ahead. With that, Pentagon planners set to work writing the actual plan for the operation. North and Moreau went over the proposed rules of engagement on a secure telephone line; even after the operation, U.S. officials refused to disclose what they were.

There were a few doubts about the wisdom of the plan. At first some State Department officials worried about the effect the operation—if successful—would have on Mubarak, walking a tightrope between moderation and a rising tide of Arab radicalism; on U.S. relations with Egypt, and on America's standing in the Arab world. Weinberger, off on a trip to Ottawa and to his summer home in Bar Harbor, Maine, was even more skittish, as was the Defense Department's representative on the counterterrorist task force, Deputy Secretary William H. Taft IV. Weinberger called the president repeatedly to express his reservations about the plan, at one point telling Reagan: "This will destroy our relations with Egypt."

In the end, the State Department argued

Continued

Sanitized Copy Approved for Release 2011/03/04 : CIA-RDP91-00587R000100080005-0

3.

McFarlane (left) and Regan with the president: Weighing the risks before ordering the attack

that the risks of hijacking the hijackers were far outweighed by the benefits—especially since the operation would relieve Mubarak of the onus of turning the Arab terrorists over to the West. Nearly all the U.S. planners agreed that if the mission were approved by the president, it would have to be kept under the tightest wraps. The security was so intense that the United States did not alert Italy.

The president ordered Weinberger to proceed, risking a major security breach in the process. Ironically, while U.S. intelligence was closely monitoring communications from Egypt, the scrambler aboard Air Force One was broken, and Reagan was forced to make his call "in the clear." As a result the conversation with Weinberger was overheard by a ham radio operator who reported that the defense secretary expressed reservations about an operation that might require Navy pilots to fire across the nose of an unarmed civilian plane. Brushing those objections aside, Reagan insisted that the mission be carried out, so long as no innocent lives were put at risk.

About 2 o'clock, or less than two hours after the president had given the green light, the plan had come together. The word was flashed to the Saratoga and the first planes—E-2C Hawkeye radar aircraft, a flight of four F-14 fighters and the Navy's EA-6B Prowler electronic warfare plane—took off and headed south to wait. But the rules of engagement had not finally been settled, and the first flight of F-14s returned to the carrier.

Shortly after 3 p.m., intelligence sources received word that 10 minutes earlier the terrorists had arrived at Al Maza Air Base. Thoughtfully, the sources also produced the terrorists' flight number. Aboard Air Force One, the president snapped, "Let's do it." At 4:13 word came that the EgyptAir plane had filed a flight plan for Algiers and taken off. Orders were instantly flashed to the Saratoga to launch its F-14s again. The chase was on.

The F-14s and their support planes, including the Hawkeyes and the Prowler electronic-warfare plane, headed to their station south of Crete and set up an airborne gate, surveying every plane headed out of Egypt until they found the EgyptAir flight they were looking for. Meanwhile, the United States set to work trying to make sure the terrorists had no place to go except into the arms of the law. President Reagan fired off a flash cable to Tunisian President Habib Bourguiba, telling him the United States had reason to believe—despite the terrorists' flight plan—that the hijackers of the Achille Lauro were aboard an EgyptAir plane headed for Tunis. The United States, Reagan said, believed the terrorists should not be allowed to land. According to one knowledgeable source, some American officials also were worried that the terrorists might try to head for Athens or Beirut; cables were sent to Greece and Lebanon after the EgyptAir flight took off, asking the governments there not to let the hijackers land.

Some 45 minutes after the EgyptAir flight took off into the darkness, it flew into the Americans' gate, 80 miles south of Crete. The Egyptian plane was right on course, flying at 34,000 feet and a speed of 400 knots. Initially the F-14s loitered behind the 737, flying without lights and with darkened cockpits. There is no evidence that anyone aboard the Egyptian jet was aware of their presence as they trailed their prey to the ambush point. Then the Americans turned on their lights and closed in alongside both wings of the airliner. "I imagine the plane informed the Egyptians when they were intercepted," Weinberger said later. But there was no evidence that the pilot had been ordered to return home.

The Egyptian pilot began desperately radioing Cairo for instructions. He tried one frequency after another, but he could not get through and he could hear only garbled sounds in his headset. The EA-6B was jamming him, jumping up and down the radio scale right along with him. Finally, reported Weinberger, the pilot "accepted the inevitable" and radioed that he would follow the American orders. The EgyptAir plane fell into place and reluctantly followed the pack of American warplanes to Sicily.

There was almost no chance the 737 would have been shot down. From the outset the president had insisted that no innocent lives were to be lost, and U.S. intelligence knew that the plane was being flown by Egyptians who had no involvement in the hijacking. Although the fighters had been authorized to fire missiles in front of the aircraft's nose, just the intimidating presence of the jets did the trick. Aboard the plane a swaggering crew of terrorists suddenly turned into cornered airborne rats. "I don't know if you ever saw a Tomcat with all its lights on going like hell," said a crewman from the Saratoga later. "It's an awesome

Veliotes (left) and Mubarak: Ambiguity about Egypt's role

Continued

4.

1. 7 p.m. local time. Off Greece in the Mediterranean, a U.S. Navy task force headed by the aircraft carrier Saratoga is ordered to prepare for a mission. It turns around and steams slowly south.

2. 8:15 p.m. Four F-14 fighters, two KA-6D air tankers and two E-2C radar planes—plus back-up planes—take off from the Saratoga and patrol north of Egypt.

3. 10:10 p.m. An Egyptian Boeing 737 carrying the hijackers takes off from Al Maza Air Base near Cairo. The E-2C Hawkeyes monitor it.

4. 11:30 p.m. The F-14s intercept the 737 in international airspace south of Crete, and a Hawkeye orders it by radio to follow them to a U.S. air base in Sicily.

5. 12:10 a.m. Refused permission to land in Tunis or Athens, the Egyptian plane obeys the order, and the F-14s escort it to the Sigonella Air Base. Italian authorities take the hijackers into custody.

sight. I guess we just scared them down."

Only when the little procession was about to enter Italian airspace did the United States inform the Italian government of its plans. To have done so earlier, although it would have been a little more diplomatic, would have risked leaks that could have killed the plan, one official said. But the Italians were less than delighted at the news. "They went crazy," says one American official. In fact, Italian ground controllers refused to grant the 737 permission to enter their airspace and the Egyptian pilot had to declare an in-flight emergency, saying he was low on fuel, in order to get clearance to land at Sigonella. When he got there, the terrorists found the commandos of SEAL Team Six, who had returned to Sicily from Gibraltar, waiting with the Italian *carabinieri*.

There was a debate over which force—the American or Italian—had jurisdiction. Secretary of State Shultz, in a long telephone conversation with Italian Foreign Minister Giulio Andreotti, yielded when Andreotti assured him the pirates would promptly be charged with murder. "We really wanted them to come home with us, but nobody is unhappy with this," said one U.S. official.

When they boarded the 737, U.S. and Italian officials found a bonus: not only had they captured the four hijackers who would be accused of seizing the Achille Lauro and murdering Leon Klinghoffer, but they found Abul Abbas, a high-ranking aide to Palestine Liberation Organization chairman Yasir Arafat. Intelligence sources believe Abbas directed the hijacking. Sources told NEWSWEEK that Abbas, a member of the PLO Executive Committee, had been in constant radio contact with the hijackers from his base in Beirut, beginning immediately after they seized the cruise ship. After the hijackers announced that they had killed one of their American hostages, the sources said, Abbas radioed them and berated them for botching their mission, which was to infiltrate Israel to carry out a terrorist operation at a military target near the port city of Ashdod. Late Friday night Abbas and an aide also on the plane were flown to Rome aboard the EgyptAir jetliner by Italian authorities.

On Saturday afternoon came the only discouraging news since the operation was launched. The United States had started extradition proceedings against Abbas but the Italians rebuffed the effort, despite a new legal-assistance treaty between the two countries. The issue was a delicate one. The Italians depend heavily on the Middle East for oil. They have close relations with the Arab world and with the PLO. And at least until recently, they have had less

Continued

5.

On the Achille Lauro, former hostages inspect the spot where Klinghoffer died: Cold blood

trouble than others from Arab terrorism.

On Saturday President Reagan sent a strongly worded letter to Italian Prime Minister Bettino Craxi in which Reagan said he was "surprised" that Italian authorities had "summarily rejected" the U.S. extradition request for Abbas, whom Reagan said had been "criminally implicated" in the hijacking of the Achille Lauro. He promised that Washington would soon deliver "overwhelming evidence" of Abbas's guilt. The mutual-assistance treaty, Reagan argued, requires the Italians to arrest Abbas and to give the United States 45 days to make its case against him. But U.S. intelligence sources reported that while American officials were trying to serve a warrant on Abbas, he apparently slipped out of Italy, dressed in an EgyptAir uniform. Leaving Rome's Fiumicino Airport on a chartered Yugoslav plane, he headed for Yugoslavia, apparently with the connivance of Italian, Egyptian and Yugoslav authorities. If the Italians collaborated in Abbas's release, they may come to regret it. "Abul Abbas has a long history of taking hostages in order to win the release of people of his who are in jail," said one U.S. official. "Now that this has happened, I'm glad the Italians are holding the terrorists, not us."

That the terrorists would ever see the inside of a jail did not seem possible in the first hours of the hijacking of the Achille Lauro. The four terrorists who seized the ship demanded that Israel release 50 Palestinian prisoners, including at least one convicted murderer; they threatened to kill the passengers they had taken captive if they didn't get their way. In the United States, the government's special worldwide antiterrorist computer network, code-named Flashboard, signaled the White House, Pentagon, State Department, CIA and National Security Agency. State Department officials set up a crisis command center to try to determine how many Americans were on the ship. They converted the emergency telephone lines that had just been used for the Mexican earthquake to handle calls from worried relatives.

Not until early Tuesday afternoon, when Syrian authorities were turning the ship away from the port of Tartus, did the full gravity of the hijacking become clear. Using highly classified eavesdropping methods, an American RC-135 spy plane learned that one of the terrorists had killed Leon Klinghoffer, 69, a New Yorker who was confined to a wheelchair. The ship's radio transmitted a grisly boast to the shore. "We threw the first body into the water after shooting him in the head," one of the pirates said. "Minutes from now we will follow up with the second one. Do not worry, Tartus, we have a lot of them here."

The four terrorists seemed more mysterious than most. It was difficult to establish who they were and what they were really after. Their target—an Italian ship—was puzzling. Italy had issued one of the sharpest criticisms of Israel's attack against PLO headquarters in Tunis, sharp enough to put a strain on relations between Jerusalem and Rome. And as the Achille Lauro plowed up and down the eastern Mediterranean, the pirates seemed a good deal more interested in getting away than in pressing their original demands.

The administration concluded that Italy and Egypt should take the lead in handling the deteriorating situation. Besides having relatively good relations with the Palestinians, Italy had a proven counterterrorist unit of at least 300 men. Among other tasks, it had rescued U.S. Brig. Gen. James Dozier from the Red Brigades. To isolate the pirates, Washington persuaded governments in the eastern Mediterranean not to allow the hijacked cruise ship to dock. The State Department also sought to rally other governments to the notion that there should be no knuckling under to terrorism and that the Israelis should hang on to their prisoners.

The administration succeeded in keeping anyone from offering the terrorists refuge, and its diplomacy ultimately led to the release of the hostages. But it did not produce the terrorists. The main problem was Mubarak, who had to secure the release of the hostages while protecting himself against the certain fury of Arab fanatics who considered the terrorists heroes. The Americans and Israelis objected violently to the man Mubarak selected as his intermediary to the terrorists: Abbas, leader of the same Palestinian splinter group to which the hijackers claimed to belong. Abbas arrived in Egypt Wednesday morning and quickly got in touch by radio with the hijackers aboard the Achille Lauro that was then anchored off Port Said. The terrorists greeted him enthusiastically. Giving orders rather than negotiating, Abbas instructed the pirates to await a boat bearing a Palestinian "with a distinguishing mark" and to accompany the man to the shore. His order was followed, and the Achille Lauro was free. While the U.S. government could not quarrel with that result, it could certainly dispute the means. The available evidence indicated that Abbas had ordered the terrorists

De Rosa: Unanswered questions

6.

Weinberger shows how it was done: The defense secretary worried about Arab reaction

on board the ship in the first place.

Mubarak and Foreign Minister Meguid argued that when they agreed to grant the terrorists safe conduct out of Egypt they were convinced that none of the Achille Lauro captives had been injured. Although the terrorists had been overheard gloating about the murder of Klinghoffer, Meguid claimed to be convinced when the ship's still captive skipper reported "Everybody is OK." The Egyptians had plenty of opportunity to learn the truth after the pirates had left the ship. But when security officials boarded the Achille Lauro at Port Said, they claimed that they were too busy looking for bombs to ask whether anyone had been killed.

Meguid said that he had learned of the murder only after he had been phoned by Italian Prime Minister Craxi, three hours after the ship had been released. By that time, Meguid said, it was too late to act upon the information: the terrorists were already out of the country. The following day Mubarak chose to blame the lapse on the Achille Lauro's skipper. "If the captain had told us that a passenger had been killed," he said, "we would have changed our position toward the whole operation." He added that the terrorists had been whisked out of the country to preserve Egypt's credibility. "We took it upon ourselves to get them out of here so that people would believe us afterwards should there be a similar operation." That, of course, was an outright lie.

Ironically, the haggling over the terrorists gave American intelligence operatives more time to discover where they were. Among other things, the operatives monitored a running debate between Egyptian and Palestinian officials over how to dispose of the hijackers. Mubarak was willing to let them go, provided that Arafat could find a country willing to accept them. From those overheard conversations, U.S. officials ultimately were able to pinpoint the location of the terrorists and to predict their movements.

Meguid had agreed that the hijackers would be given safe passage out of the country. The decision enraged U.S. Ambassador Veliotes, who on an open radio transmission from the Achille Lauro instructed a subordinate to "tell the foreign minister that we demand that they prosecute these sons of bitches." Instead, Meguid announced that the terrorists had been permitted to flee Egypt.

U.S. intelligence agencies keeping watch on the Tunisian coast reported that despite the Egyptian claims, the terrorists had not turned up at the PLO's refuge. The American fury at Mubarak grew. His aides argued with Veliotes that a small country like Egypt should not be forced to go out on a limb to fight terrorism when the major powers had refused to confront the problem. "The Egyptians were no help at all," said one senior U.S. official.

Convinced that the terrorists were still in Egyptian jurisdiction, Veliotes declared: "These are murderers, and there should be an investigation and they should be prosecuted according to the laws of Egypt like any other criminals." According to informed sources, the terrorists were seen with Abbas in Cairo's Sheraton Heliopolis Hotel many hours after they were said to have fled. The transparent conclusion was that even after the murder was established, the Egyptians meant to sneak the terrorists out of the country in the company of the very man who may have ordered their piratical act.

Feelings became harder when the Egyptians detained the ship even as they appeared to be letting the terrorists escape. But all along there was enough ambiguity to Cairo's moves to convince some that Mubarak did not mean for the terrorists to get off scot free. According to a well-placed congressional source, officials of the Egyptian intelligence service quietly passed on precise information about the EgyptAir flight. Others including Reagan said the United States had acted alone.

Earlier, New York Republican Sen. Alfonse D'Amato expressed the view of many of his congressional colleagues when he called for taking a harder look at Egypt's more than $2 billion a year in U.S. military and economic aid. But such talk was considerably muted once it was learned that Egypt may have supplied Washington with covert intelligence. According to one Senate source, it's easy to understand why Mubarak acted as he did: he clearly understood the risk to Egypt's relations with the United States. Egypt is second only to Israel in the amount of U.S. foreign aid it receives. But he was also aware of the danger he faced from Egyptian and other Arab radicals. The Egyptians remember all too well what happened to the late Anwar Sadat. Now, however, Mubarak can claim he never gave in to American pressure and still maintain correct relations with Washington.

Abul Abbas: The hijackers were his men

The success of the ambush helped ease earlier frictions. And the administration clearly had no intention of breaking with a vital strategic partner. "As of this morning," said a congressional source after the interception, "you're not going to find any American official attacking Egypt in public the way they did yesterday." How much sportsmanship Egypt would show remained an open question. Initially at least, Mubarak accused the United States of piracy in seizing the Egyptian air-

7

liner. And Cairo rumbled with anti-American bitterness.

At one point NEWSWEEK'S Rod Nordland was surrounded by a crowd of angry students. "Are you American?" they shouted, pressing in close, shaking their fists, pulling at his clothes and tearing pages from his notebook. "I thought it wise to lie," he reported. "I'm French," he said, and the mood immediately cooled. Then other voices shouted, "He looks like an American," and "He's probably an Israeli spy."

"You'd better get out of here fast," counseled the single sympathetic voice in the mob. Suddenly, however, a triple line of police began to charge. To Nordland's relief, the anti-American mob broke up and fled. An armored car charged through the scattering ranks firing dozens of tear-gas canisters into the crowd. One student ran up to him and shook a hot canister in his face. "See what your country is doing to us," he said, pointing to the inscription that read "Made in U.S.A."

With feelings souring, the released American hostages flew from Cairo to Sicily on a U.S. military jet. At the Italian section of the Sigonella Air Base, the four hijackers were mustered for a lineup. Four of the passengers were led in separately to identify them. "There was positive, unequivocal identification," said Frank Hodes, one of the released Americans. "I saw them as they came out [of the lineup]," said his wife, Mildred. "And there was no doubt that it was the same men." The former hostages, added Hodes, "were elated, euphoric that they had the guys who created this world incident and caused the death of a very dear friend of ours."

Back home the sense of jubilation was also stronger than anxiety over what might happen next in the ongoing war against terrorism. "Thank God," exclaimed New York Sen. Daniel Patrick Moynihan. "We've finally won one." Ronald Reagan placed a phone call to Marilyn Klinghoffer, the widow of Achille Lauro's helpless, innocent martyr. According to her son-in-law, she thanked the president for his condolences, saying: "I just want you to know how much the terrorists hate you." "I appreciate that," Reagan responded, "but I hope they'll have more reason to hate me in the future as we continue to try to stop these people from committing these terrible acts." "These people don't deserve to live," said Mrs. Klinghoffer with rising bitterness. "They are despicable! Late last night in Italy I had the opportunity to face every one of them. I spat in their faces and I told them what I thought of them."

"You did?" exclaimed the president. "God bless you."

JOHN WALCOTT with ROD NORDLAND in Cairo, THEODORE STANGER in Rome, MILAN J. KUBIC in Jerusalem, ANDREW NAGORSKI in Bonn, JOHN BARRY in Washington and SUSAN AGREST in New York

STAT

Sanitized Copy Approved for Release 2011/03/04 : CIA-RDP91-00587R000100080005-0

Made in the USA
Lexington, KY
14 December 2019

58562457R00148